The Marriage Maker

JOHN & TERI NIEDER

HARVEST HOUSE PUBLISHERS
Eugene, Oregon 97402

Cover design by Terry Dugan Design, Minneapolis, Minnesota

THE MARRIAGE MAKER

Copyright ©1996 by John and Teri Nieder

Published by Harvest House Publishers
Eugene, Oregon 97402

Library of Congress Cataloging-in-Publication Data

Nieder, John
    The marriage maker / John and Teri Nieder.
        p. cm.
    ISBN 1-56507-333-9
    1. Marriage—Religious aspects—Christianity. 2. Holy Spirit. 3. Married people—Religious life. I. Nieder, Teri. II. Title.
    BV835.N546   1996
248.8'44—dc20   96–14508
                                                CIP

Acknowledgments

We would like to express our heartfelt appreciation to the following people:

To Bob Hawkins, Jr., Carolyn McCready, Betty Fletcher, and the entire Harvest House team for being both professional and incredibly gracious.

To Larry Weeden for using your gifts to make our words come alive.

To our children, JT, Katie, and Erik, who have each paid a high price so this book could be completed.

Contents

While this book is a team effort, for ease of reading it is written in John's voice. To capture her unique perspective as a woman, wife, and mother, Teri's comments are italicized.

God's Extraordinary Provision

What if God, the almighty Creator of the universe and of all life, including yours and ours, were willing to walk with you moment by moment through each day? What if He were willing to be your personal Counselor, guiding *and* empowering you, helping you to have a satisfying, joy-filled marriage? And what if, to make all this possible, He were willing to take up residence *inside* you, spending 24 hours of every day in intimate relationship with you?

Well, one of the most incredibly amazing truths of the Christian life is that you don't have to imagine any of these things. If you have trusted in Jesus Christ as your Savior, *God is willing,* and *He has already come to live inside you* to give you this kind of life in the person of the Holy Spirit.

The Holy Spirit is not a mystical, unknowable force. And He's certainly not just a part of the church's past. He is, in fact, essential to the fulfillment of God's purposes in our lives today.

If this is true, why doesn't the experience of most Christians reflect His presence? If He wants to be our marriage Counselor, why do Christians get divorced just about as often as nonbelievers? And why would many Christians, if you asked them what God would have them do when they're in the middle of a conflict with their spouse, be able to give only a vague answer?

As we've seen in our own marriage, and in talking and working with hundreds of other couples, the reason is simply that most of us haven't begun to understand and appropriate the ministry of the Holy Spirit in our lives. He wants to be and do so much for us, but we frequently miss His messages. We enjoy only a fraction of the help He wants to give, and we live on a far lower plane than God desires and intends for us.

Learning more about the Spirit, seeking and getting His guidance, and drawing on His strength for Christlike living in our marriage—these have been the keys to the survival of our relationship. They are also responsible for our thriving marriage today. Yes, we've had our rocky periods. At one time early on, though we were in a ministry to families and people assumed we had a great marriage, we were actually in deep trouble. But thanks to the Spirit's working in each of us and in our relationship, we can honestly say that now, after more than 20 years of marriage, our life together has never been better.

Who is the Holy Spirit? What difference can He really make in our daily lives and in our marriages? The answer is, "All the difference in the world." So let's take a closer look at the Holy Spirit at work.

1

We Really Needed Help

On fire for God. Driven. Consumed. I was so excited that I literally couldn't sleep. I was completing my seminary studies when an unlikely meeting with Dr. Howard Hendricks turned out to be a divine appointment. He told me that he and his wife, Jeanne, had been praying for years that some of their students would minister God's Word through the electronic media. Tears came to my eyes. Their prayer was my vision! Suddenly my days and nights were filled with the myriad details involved in launching a nationwide radio program.

At home, my wife, Teri, was pregnant and really excited about becoming a mom. Since she seemed to be doing okay, I crossed the pregnancy off my "to do" list. My days were full, and I was learning new things about Christian radio all the time—and I was enjoying every minute of it!

But I didn't see that Teri and I were growing apart....

⟨∞⟩

I was really excited about the new radio program, but even more, I was thrilled by the prospect of having our baby. I had wanted children ever since I was a little girl. And since it had taken us a while to get pregnant, my anticipation grew daily. Yet suddenly, as John got wrapped up in preparing for the broadcast, it seemed that everything else in his life—including me and our baby—took second place. A distant second place.

As I battled morning sickness and tried to get the nursery together and decorated, I grew anxious and a bit depressed. Then my due date approached and passed in early January. "I want to hold this baby in the worst way," I told John.

⟨∞⟩

Teri finally got her chance late in the evening of January 21, after 27 hours of horrible back labor. Watching her go through that pain, I remember feeling guilty. *I don't know how she can stand it!* I thought. *And I caused it!*

All that was temporarily forgotten, however, when we welcomed John Thomas (J.T. as we came to call him) into the world. We both gave thanks and dedicated him to the Lord that night. A few days later, we took him home.

⟨∞⟩

The tension in our relationship escalated dramatically the day we all got home. I was still in a lot of pain, and John had to help me do something as simple as get out of bed. When I

*tried to do it on my own that afternoon, I began to hemor-
rhage profusely. John was standing there when it happened.*

❧

I thought I was going to watch her bleed to death in
front of my eyes. The paramedics came and took her to
the hospital, and we survived that crisis. But then came
the daily grind of a baby who wanted to sleep only one
or two hours a night, and who was colicky as well. In addition, I found I couldn't satisfy the baby. When he cried,
which was most of the time, I just handed him to Teri.

After a few sleepless nights, I grew desperate for es-
cape so I could get enough rest to finish preparing the
broadcast. I still had a lot of work to do before our first
program aired in just a couple of days. (Giving birth twice
in two weeks is not a good idea.)

❧

*I was feeling the same fatigue and frustration John was.
I wanted so badly to comfort J.T., but his colic made that impossible. He just cried and cried. And when John got away
as he figured he had to, I felt abandoned.*

❧

The ministry got off to a good start, with more than
a thousand letters coming in response to the first week
of broadcasts. I became more wrapped up in my work
than ever. Letters and tapes filled our tiny garage and

overflowed into our living room and kitchen. All I did was work. I had little time for the Lord, let alone Teri. Our marriage took an even steeper turn downhill.

∞

The initial response to the ministry only aggravated the problems in our marriage—and John was too busy to even notice. All I could do was try to handle the baby by myself and not get John upset. He would be on the phone, and the baby would start crying again, and no matter what I did, he wouldn't stop. At times John would get angry, and I felt so helpless and alone.

I was also deeply perplexed and frustrated by the contradiction in our lives. On the one hand, I saw God using John in the ministry and making that grow. But on the other, I saw that our relationship with Him was deteriorating even as our marriage withered. I was sure God would not honor the ministry long-term without a change in our personal lives.

This went on for weeks and then months. Our relationship was a mess; I felt helpless and hopeless; and John didn't know any of this.

∞

I lived for my work—18 hours a day of it—and not much else. I assumed we were okay. But Teri knew we were not.

∞

We couldn't continue much longer the way we were going. The few times I tried to say something, John quickly shut me down. When I would start to cry, he walked away. I felt like I was on the verge of a nervous breakdown. If things went on as they were much longer, I sensed I would lose my mind, not to mention my marriage.

The whole situation finally came to a head one day when I reached my limit and started to cry for no apparent reason. Through my tears I told John, "We need to get help. We have to see a counselor."

❦

As she said those words, she began to tremble uncontrollably.

Her words hit me like a sledgehammer between the eyes. I knew I had been ignoring her, but now I couldn't overlook her pain. *Hypocrite!* I thought. *Here you are directing a ministry to couples and families, and your own home is in shambles.*

But, once again, I responded poorly. I got angry, shut her out, and walked away.

A day or so later, the situation went from bad to worse. Because nothing had been resolved yet, we had both been stewing in our anger. Then it came spewing out in a major fight. Teri, shall we say, pointed out some of my shortcomings in a way that hurt me.

I totally lost it. I blurted out the words I knew would do the most to hurt her back: "Do you just want to get a divorce?" I demanded.

In the heat of the moment, my heart was cold. I really didn't care what I said or did. And, God forgive me, in my anger I wanted more than anything to hurt her. I succeeded all too well.

I've never felt so hurt, afraid, and insecure as I did at that moment. For days afterward, all I could do was take care of the baby, cry, and pray. I really didn't know how things were going to turn out. My prayers were cries of desperation. I was physically and emotionally exhausted. I knew the Lord was not pleased with us, but I also knew He still cared.

I knew I was in the wrong, but emotionally I just didn't care. I knew *that* was wrong, too. And I couldn't deny any longer that all the warmth and tender feelings between us were gone. In a quiet moment, I prayed, "Lord, please help me. Please help *us.*"

I found myself wondering how this situation could have happened. We were both believers. We wanted to live our lives for the Lord. How did we grow so distant from Him and from each other?

You see, our relationship was an example of something all too common in churches, ministries, families, and certainly Christian marriages. We were operating without the personal involvement of the Holy Spirit in our marriage.

To Help You Pray

At the close of a number of chapters, we are including prayers to help you cultivate your relationship with the Holy Spirit. Whenever possible, read these biblically based prayers out loud. There is spiritual power in the spoken Word of God (Ephesians 6:17,18).

Heavenly Father,

I confess that in many ways I live my life apart from You. I get busy and forget how much I need You in my life. Forgive me for the times that I have not made You the priority of my life.

Father, I want to take an honest look at my life and my marriage. May the Holy Spirit be my Counselor. Show me anything that I am doing that stands in the way of having a marriage that centers on the person of Your Son. Show me how I can be guided and empowered by the Holy Spirit so that the Lord Jesus Christ will be glorified in my life.

I ask this in His name. Amen.

2

The Incredible Difference

Teri and I have spent a lot of time reflecting on what took place between us, and we now realize we were losing a spiritual battle for our marriage. In subtle ways, we were beginning to look for our sense of purpose, fulfillment, and identity apart from our relationship with the Lord. Teri was looking to her role as a wife and mother, while I was finding my identity in my work and ministry.

In retrospect, we also suspect that anger and bitterness had given ground to the enemy, who hates everything for which our life and ministry stand. Despite my excellent seminary training, Teri and I didn't really understand that apart from Christ and the ministry of the Holy Spirit, we could not win this battle.

Now it's our firm belief—and the central thesis of this book—that the Holy Spirit can make an incredible difference in the daily life of a marriage. He *wants* to strengthen, guide, and in all ways improve our marriages. Jesus described Him as "another Counselor to be with you forever—the Spirit of truth" (John 14:16,17).

But if that's all true (and, of course, it is), what would His help look like in our everyday experience? Specifically, how might the Holy Spirit have made a difference in our troubled marriage so that neither Teri nor I would have feared for the future of our relationship? Let's explore how things *might* have gone if we had been more open to His leading.

⌗

Like so many men, I tend to be driven. When I set my mind to do something (like start a new radio ministry), I can't rest until it's done. I lose sight of everyone and everything else and just keep pushing, pushing, pushing. My priorities get all out of order. Even my relationship with God can take a backseat to the work I'm doing for Him.

The Holy Spirit, being God, knows these things about me. Consistent with God's Word, He wanted to challenge my work-dominated lifestyle, point out my misplaced priorities, remind me that my relationship with Him is more important than my service, and show me how I was neglecting to meet my wife's legitimate and increasingly desperate needs.

⌗

Although I was supportive of the new ministry, I was focused first on my desire to have a baby, then on taking care of him after he was born. I didn't understand the tremendous weight of responsibility John felt to get the radio program up and running and, at the same time, provide financially for our growing family.

I had also allowed my relationship with the Lord to stagnate. I wasn't doing what I could to study the Word of God and help myself grow and be more like Him. I prayed for my marriage to change, for John and the baby to change, but I didn't pray for me *to change.*

The Holy Spirit knew these things and wanted to help me be more aware of and sensitive to the pressures John was feeling. When he got anxious or angry, the Spirit wanted me to understand that John was responding not so much to me as to his own fear and insecurity. When I felt concern for the state of our marriage, the Spirit wanted me to be bold enough to confront John in love much sooner than I did (before I had reached the end of my emotional rope). And He certainly wanted me to move beyond just existing spiritually. He wanted me to start growing again in my Christian walk. He wanted me to understand that my ultimate fulfillment would not be found in my roles of wife or mother, but rather in my relationship with the Lord.

For a long time I went on trying to do everything in my own strength. As a result, I was feeling overwhelmed and was cracking under the pressure. I was trying to ignore the most fundamental fact of daily Christian life— "apart from me [Jesus] you can do nothing" (John 15:5). The enemy was having his way, and I didn't even know it. The Holy Spirit, however, was working through my circumstances to break down my pride and force me to realize just how inadequate I am on my own.

When Teri had finally reached her limit and we had that verbal confrontation described in chapter 1, my self-empowered approach to life was laid bare. You see, I've always had a quick tongue and a sharp wit. I've "won" nearly every verbal battle Teri and I have ever fought. In the book of James, we're warned about the tongue's capacity to light a fire in another person's spirit, and I've provided the proof of that on many occasions. So when we got into it that day, since I was doing everything on my own, I didn't hesitate to pull out my "big gun"—the threat of divorce—when she said some things that hurt me. Even though I knew I would never pursue a divorce, I also knew that just the mention of it would hurt her deeply, and that was my goal in that terrible moment.

If I had been in touch with the Holy Spirit at that point, before I lost my temper and let loose with my tongue, I believe He would have "stepped between" me and Teri, urged me to think hard about what I was going to say next, and offered to strengthen me to do the right thing. In fact, I believe He was right there with us, trying to tell me those things—but I wasn't listening.

❦

In my own way, I wasn't listening, either. After all, it takes two to fight.

If both of us had been listening better, I still would have needed to say some hard things to John about his priorities and lifestyle. But under the Spirit's direction, I could have said them more tenderly and lovingly—in a way that didn't make John immediately defensive.

❧

And I, also under the Spirit's direction, could have determined to think about what she said before responding. Even if I were tempted to pull out my big gun, I could have heard the quiet, inner voice of the Spirit saying, *No, that's not right. It's not fair to her, and besides, you made a pledge to never consider divorce.*

But even though the Spirit was there, willing and able to intervene, we were not sensitive to His presence and therefore didn't turn to Him for help.

❧

If we had, the whole situation could have been handled much better. We could have dealt with the issues—our different priorities, John's workaholism, and so on—much sooner and more pleasantly and never reached a crisis point. Working things out still would have been hard—these were tough issues, after all. But our entire approach and the atmosphere in our home could have been so much more healthy.

❧

Instead, however, we had to learn our lessons the more difficult way. Because we weren't listening very well to the Spirit, He got our attention through our circumstances, through the consequences of our words and actions. When

I pulled out my verbal big gun and fired it, the devastating results forced me to see how overwhelmed, self-willed, and out of control I had become. I was compelled to face the truth of Teri's concerns. My inadequacy was now painfully clear.

In other words, though we didn't handle the situation nearly as well as we could have had we been listening to and submitting to the Holy Spirit, He was still at work in each of us individually and in our relationship together. That's the truth of Philippians 1:6: "Being confident of this, that he who began a good work in you *will* carry it on to completion until the day of Christ Jesus" (emphasis added).

Looking back on our own struggle, we now realize that self-confidence stands in the way of our seeking the ministry of the Holy Spirit. The Holy Spirit can only do His work when we fully acknowledge how desperately we need Him. We must also believe that the Holy Spirit can and will control us, if only we ask Him.

∽∾

There's a lot more to be said about the difference the Holy Spirit could have made in our marriage up to that point—and has made since. We'll be adding details of that story throughout this book, but the bottom line is this: Our marriages are a work of God. Because God is so committed to "growing us up" spiritually, and because He gave us the Holy Spirit as our Counselor to help accomplish that, we need to understand just how that works. Specifically, we will look at how a husband and wife can come under the control of the Spirit so their relationship will honor the Savior and bring them the joy and satisfaction God intends for marriage.

We've started that look with the story of a time when our marriage was far from God's intention. Now, in the next chapter, we'll paint a picture of what constitutes the "normal" Christian marriage when the Holy Spirit is given free rein in both spouses' lives.

Heavenly Father,

Thank You for the gift of the Holy Spirit. I long for Him to be my Counselor, my Helper, and my ever-present Friend. I realize that apart from the ministry of the Holy Spirit I cannot live the Christian life. Please teach me to hear His voice and to follow His directions. Help me to understand the depth of my need for the Spirit's work in my life and in my marriage.

I ask this in Jesus' name. Amen.

3

Living the Life
Together

Andy and Carol have been married for more than 15
years. They're active in their church and are part of
the leadership team for the junior high ministry. The dedicated parents of two soon-to-be-teens, they appear to have
the perfect family.

Recently, however, Carol has grown emotionally de-
tached. She doesn't feel loved, wanted, or appreciated by
Andy or the children. "I've given and given to them over
the years," she told me. "I just don't have anything more
to give. Now I don't seem to care anymore."

Not surprisingly, she has entertained serious thoughts
about divorce.

Steve and Jennifer were made for each other, everyone
said. At the time of their wedding, he had just finished an
outstanding college career, leading his basketball team to

a regional title. Jennifer, a beautiful young woman, had excelled in college and planned to become a teacher. Less than two years later, however, their marriage had become a battlefield, and their future was in grave doubt.

Soon after their honeymoon, Jennifer discovered that Steve's temper is a daily land mine, exploding on a moment's notice. "At first, I tried to avoid doing anything that might set him off, but it didn't work," she told their pastor (unbeknownst to Steve). "Eventually, I responded by becoming just as hot-headed myself."

She continued, "Something has to change. Our marriage won't survive much more of this."

Rick knew his wife, Bridget, wasn't happy, but he never expected her to be unfaithful. She was the mother of their three children and an immaculate housekeeper. She had taught a first-grade Sunday school class for years and was adored by her students.

Then one day she announced to Rick, "I've found a man who makes me feel loved and appreciated. I want out of our marriage." Rick's feelings didn't matter, and neither did the devastation she had brought on their kids.

Unfortunately, the struggles of these three couples are typical of today's Christian marriages. When you look at the divorce statistics, you see there's little difference between the survival rates of Christian and non-Christian unions. Why is that? If a husband and wife are both believers in Jesus Christ, shouldn't their personal relationship with the God of the Universe make a difference in their marriage? Shouldn't they have a "leg up" on the rest of the world?

If we, as individuals and married couples, were living what God intends to be normal Christian lives, in tune with the Counselor He sent us to guide and empower us, our marriages would be setting us apart from the rest of the world.

In a word, yes. So why are so many Christian marriages in trouble; and why do so many end in the tragedy of divorce? The answer is amazingly simple, but with profound implications. From our own years of marriage and counseling with other couples, we are convinced that most Christians today do not understand how God wants to accomplish His work in our lives and in our homes. As a result, we have mediocre lives and mediocre marriages that are, indeed, little different from those of our unsaved friends.

If we, as individuals and married couples, were living what God intends to be normal Christian lives, in tune with the Counselor He sent to guide and empower us, our marriages *would* be setting us apart from the rest of the world. We would experience far more healthy and, when necessary, healed families, and far fewer divorces. In fact, the Holy Spirit wants our marriages to be a reflection of His power and His presence. We would enjoy what God intends for our relationships.

What Is the Normal Christian Life?

What should this normal Christian life and marriage be? The answer isn't hard to find; it's spelled out in the Bible. We could look at many passages that come at the subject from distinct perspectives, but let's consider just a few to start.

In the book of Galatians, the apostle Paul made the point to his readers that they were no longer required to obey the Jewish law first given to Moses. Instead, they (and we) were free to—and should—live by faith, under the direction of the Holy Spirit. And what qualities would the Spirit produce in those yielded to Him? What would be the fruit of His work in their lives?

Paul listed those distinctives in chapter 5: "The fruit of the Spirit is love, joy, peace, patience, kindness, good-ness, faithfulness, gentleness, and self-control" (verses 22,23). If we're living as God intends, the Spirit will be de-veloping these qualities in us, and they will be clearly vis-ible in our lives and marriages. But if we don't walk in the Spirit, we will naturally walk in the power of the flesh, or sin, which produces sexual immorality, relational hostility, and emotions such as anger and bitterness (see verses 19-21).

Notice that the very first thing we should see is love. Jesus said the same thing when He identified the trait that would mark us as His disciples: "A new command I give you: Love one another. As I have loved you, so you must love one another. By this all men will know that you are my disciples, if you love one another" (John 13:34,35). And immediately after that He talked about the coming of the

Holy Spirit. This unique capacity to love is made possible by the Holy Spirit's work in us.

We are to love one another as the Savior loves us—sacrificially, without condition, putting the other person's needs ahead of our own. That's not easy, to say the least, but that's the kind of love the Spirit wants to produce in us and in our relationships.

Next, the normal Christian life should be characterized by joy. "Be joyful always," Paul said. Even when things aren't going as well as we'd like, we can have a deep, abiding joy in the Lord when we're walking through each day with the Spirit.

The next character quality is peace. If there's anything that people in our culture seem to need, it's this. So few of us, including Christians, appear to have it. Yet it's a natural part of the Spirit's effective presence in our lives. In fact, immediately after Jesus gave the promise of the coming of the Spirit in John 14, He added, "Peace I leave with you; my peace I give you. I do not give to you as the world gives. Do not let your hearts be troubled and do not be afraid" (verse 27). It's God's peace, a divine peace. Only He can give it—but that's exactly what He wants to do through His indwelling Spirit. So we have peace with God, which allows us to have peace with each other.

Patience is another part of the Spirit's fruit and another mark of the normal Christian life and marriage. In the famous "love chapter," 1 Corinthians 13, the apostle Paul first talked about the importance of love. Then in verse 4 he began to describe love, and the first thing he said was, "Love is patient"—it suffers long in relation to the actions of another.

When we and our spouse aren't seeing eye to eye, or when our spouse does his or her annoying habit for at least the thousandth time, how do we respond? If the Spirit is in control, we respond patiently.

We also respond with kindness. "Love is kind" was Paul's very next description in 1 Corinthians 13:4. It has been said, and is too often true, that we tend to treat strangers better than we treat the members of our own families, including our spouse. If we were to ask your spouse whether you treat him or her kindly, what answer would we get? If you're like us, there are times when the answer would be painful to hear. Yet here again, kindness is part of what the Spirit is eager to produce in our individual lives and in our marriages.

Our lives are also to be marked by goodness. This quality, like all those that make up the fruit of the Spirit, mirrors the nature of God Himself. As Psalm 34:8 tells us, "Taste and see that the LORD is good." Goodness means praiseworthy character and moral excellence. Would those around you say you have those? Would your spouse? If the Spirit is allowed to work in you, you'll have them more and more.

Faithfulness is the next part of the Spirit's fruit. It means dependability and loyalty. It means that when we say we'll do something, we do it. It means that even in those times when we don't particularly like our spouse, we still keep our vows, including the one to protect our marriage bed. Deuteronomy 7:9 describes God as "the faithful God, keeping his covenant of love to a thousand generations of those who love him and keep his commands." His people, in turn, are to be called "the faithful" (Psalm 31:23).

Like the other dimensions of the fruit of the Spirit, this one isn't easy. In fact, only the Spirit can develop faithfulness in us. And that's exactly what He wants to do.

Gentleness, another characteristic of the normal Christian life and marriage, isn't one we're always eager to seek, especially those of us who are men. That's because men usually equate it with weakness, which they definitely don't want. But that's *not* what the Bible has in mind when it tells us, for example, "Let your gentleness be evident to all" (Philippians 4:5).

Biblically, gentleness means "power under control." Think of a huge, powerful horse, able to pull a heavy wagon for miles. There's tremendous energy, enormous strength there. But it's under control; it's not running wild, going off in every direction, doing more harm than good. It's harnessed, productive, being used for a positive purpose.

That's the kind of gentleness the Spirit brings forth in those who are yielded to Him.

Our Christian lives and relationships should be characterized by self-control. As I have said before, when under a lot of pressure, I have at times been impatient and insensitive with Teri. If ever there's a clear sign that I'm not in touch with the Spirit, that's it. But He has been working in me in this area, and I can honestly say that with His help, I've been doing much better in recent years. In fact, I wouldn't mind if you asked Teri to confirm that statement!

And finally, there is self-control. The dramatic increase in sexual sins and divorce among Christians in recent years is, in part, testimony to the decline in self-control in the church. Especially in today's sex-saturated and me-first culture, self-control is difficult. But that's no surprise to God. The writer of Proverbs recognized both the importance and the challenge of self-control when he wrote, "He who is slow to anger is better than the mighty, and he who rules his spirit, than he who captures a city" (Proverbs 16:32, NASB).

Once again, only the Spirit can develop that kind of self-control in us as we relate to each other in marriage. And that's what He will do, more and more, as we cooperate with Him.

Christ Living in Us

But how does it happen? How does the Holy Spirit transform our lives so that we experience love, joy, peace and all the other relational delights in our lives?

Paul gave us the answer in Galatians 2:20 when he wrote, "I have been crucified with Christ and I no longer live, but Christ lives in me. The life I live in the body, I live by faith in the Son of God, who loved me and gave himself for me." When we see ourselves as having died with Christ and we put to death our own desires, our own agenda, the Holy Spirit begins to reproduce the life of Christ in us. When we surrender control of our lives to the Holy Spirit, He magnifies Jesus Christ in us, and then we begin to relate to others the way our Savior does. In essence, the fruit of the Holy Spirit is the product of Christ living His life through us as we respond to the leading and empowering of the Holy Spirit.

When Jesus promised the Counselor, He was telling His disciples that His very life would be made real in them by the ministry of the Holy Spirit.

Now you have an overview of what the normal Christian life and marriage should be like—the quality of life God intends for us, and what the Holy Spirit wants to produce. How well does your marriage match up to that description now? How much more would you like it to?

We trust you would appreciate having a lot more of the fruit of the Spirit in your personal life (that's where it starts) and in your relationship with your spouse. So let's turn our attention now to gaining a better understanding of just *who* the Spirit is and *how* he wants to work in and through us.

Heavenly Father,

I want to experience the full measure of the Spirit's work in my life and in my relationship with _____ (spouse). Fill me with Your Holy Spirit so that I may live a life of love, joy, peace, patience, goodness, kindness, gentleness, faithfulness, and self-control.

In the Savior's name. Amen.

4

The Spirit
Is a Person

Before I became a Christian, I was any parents' worst
nightmare as a date for their daughter. I indulged in
what I call "casual hedonism." I was totally self-centered,
and one of my main forms of communication was the sarcastic barb. When Christians talked to me about their faith,
I would sometimes chide them or take delight in pointing
out some way in which they seemed like hypocrites.

Finally, however, after an intense six months of struggling with the idea of becoming a Christian, I trusted in
Jesus as my Savior. When I did, the result was an immediate and dramatic change. My self-centered isolationism
was replaced by a desire to love and be loved. My quick
tongue suddenly had a master who wouldn't tolerate my
sarcastic barbs. My "live for today" attitude gave way to
a commitment to live for the eternal. While I still needed
to grow in many areas, I had become a man who could

love his wife as Jesus loves the church (see Ephesians 5:25). What accounts for the instant and incredible changes in my heart and mind?

Our friends Earl and Sally were already married and on the verge of divorce when they became Christians. Sally was fed up with Earl's being gone for days on end. And when he was home, he hardly acknowledged her. After she finally told him she wanted out of the marriage, he approached it as just another business decision. When the neighbors heard about the separation, they weren't the least bit surprised. After all, they had been listening to the screams from Earl and Sally's home for several years.

About that time, a couple of women invited Sally to a Bible study. The emotional pain filling her life opened her heart to the gospel. Following one of the studies, Sally sat with a few of the other women and placed her trust in the Savior. Immediately, she began to pray for Earl.

Her prayers were soon answered. Earl was on a plane for a business trip and "just happened" to sit next to a man who has been used by God to bring thousands of people to a saving relationship with Jesus. There on the plane, Earl, the prominent and previously cold-hearted businessman, bowed his head and asked Jesus to be his Savior and Lord.

Having been personally transformed, Earl and Sally both set about changing their marriage. With the love of God filling their hearts, they started to share that love with each other and become one in Christ. By the time we met them some years later, the strength and beauty of their relationship were such that it was hard to believe they had ever been ready to walk away from their marriage.

What could produce such a sudden and amazing transformation in a marriage? Actually, the answer isn't a what but a *who*. And the who is the Holy Spirit.

The "Person" Behind the Name

The Bible teaches that God has revealed Himself in three distinct persons—Father, Son, and Holy Spirit—yet God is one. We call this doctrine the Trinity, and understanding it completely is beyond the ability of human reason. In this book, we're concentrating on the third person of the Trinity, who is easily the most misunderstood.

Because the Holy Spirit is God, He's with us all the time, whether we acknowledge His presence or not, whether we choose to ignore Him or to appropriate His counsel and His power for godly living.

It's important to realize first that the Spirit is God. Genesis 1:1, for example, tells us, "In the beginning God created the heavens and the earth." That's a well-known passage that establishes God as the originator of the universe and all that's in it, including human life. But how did He do the work of creation? We get an indication later in the same verse: "the Spirit of God was hovering over the waters."

God created; the Spirit of God was there doing the work. The Spirit is God. And as such, He knows all and can do all. Nothing escapes His attention, and no task is beyond His power to perform. Further, God is working out His sovereign plan—He's not our servant, taking orders from us or being manipulated by us. He is the unseen deity in our midst.

Because the Holy Spirit is God, He's with us all the time, whether we acknowledge His presence or not, whether we choose to ignore Him or to appropriate His counsel and His power for godly living. We can't hide from Him by pretending He isn't there, like a child covering his eyes with his hands and saying, "You can't see me!" He's with us in the bedroom, in the family room, and in the midst of conflict when we're tempted to say something hurtful that's better left unsaid.

Second, we need to understand that the Spirit is a person, not some vague or impersonal force. We know this because the Bible gives us many examples of His personhood. Romans 8:27, for instance, tells us He has a mind and is intelligent. He makes decisions, such as what spiritual gifts are given to which Christians (see 1 Corinthians 12:11).

Notice, too, that the Spirit has emotions. He can be grieved by or disappointed in us if we don't rid our lives of bitterness, anger, and slander against others (see Ephesians 4:30,31). For a married couple, that means we grieve the Spirit if we carry grudges, don't forgive each other, or if we verbally abuse each other. And remember from chapter 3 the fruit He wants to produce in our lives—including peace and joy—qualities that He Himself possesses.

Since the Holy Spirit is a person, He can be obeyed (see, for example, Acts 10:19-21), opposed (see Acts 7:51), insulted (see Hebrews 10:28,29), and even lied to (see Acts 5:3)—not that our lies would ever succeed in fooling Him. He also teaches us (see John 14:26), guides and directs us (see Romans 8:14), gives us strength and power (see Ephesians 3:16), and even prays for us (see Romans 8:26).

Because the Spirit is a person, we can have a relationship with Him. We sometimes struggle with that idea, however. How can we relate to someone who has no physical body? Perhaps an analogy will help.

I host a radio program. People all over the country hear my voice every day. They may listen to a tape of one of our broadcasts, read an article or a book I've written, or write to our ministry headquarters and get a response from me. Most of the listeners have never seen me, but they know there's a person behind the voice and the writings. By our interaction, we have a relationship.

In a similar way, though we never see the Holy Spirit, we know He exists as a person. We can have a relationship with Him. We can talk with Him in prayer, sharing our problems and concerns, as well as our hopes and dreams. We can learn more about Him by reading the Bible He inspired (see 2 Peter 1:21). And we can see His leading in our lives (we'll talk about that in the next chapter).

Incredibly, this person who is God *lives inside each of us* who has trusted in Jesus as Savior! The Bible teaches this truth in a number of places. For example: "Do you not know that your body is a temple of the Holy Spirit, who is in you, whom you have received from God?"

(1 Corinthians 6:19). That was written to ordinary believers—to all believers.

It is when we allow the Holy Spirit to be our primary teacher that our lives will truly be transformed. We must reach the point where we are more concerned about what the Spirit says than what any well-known Christian leader says.

An Amazing Transformation

Jesus, just a few hours before His death, talked about the coming of the Holy Spirit into our world. The Holy Spirit's ultimate goal is to bring honor and glory to Jesus Christ. He accomplishes this in several ways. First, Jesus said, "When he comes, he will convict the world of guilt in regard to sin" (John 16:8). In other words, He works in the hearts and minds of people to show them their need for a Savior, their need for the forgiveness of God that's available through the cross. If you're not yet a Christian, the Spirit wants to speak to you about that even now. When I struggled for six months with the idea of trusting in Jesus, it was the Spirit who drew me to Him. Likewise with Earl and Sally, the Spirit spoke to their minds and hearts, leading them to salvation. *He can and will do the same for you, if only you'll listen.*

Second, once we become Christians the Holy Spirit wants to enter our lives and be our Counselor moment by moment. Jesus said, "I will ask the Father, and he will give you another Counselor to be with you forever—the Spirit of truth" (John 14:16,17). By "another," Jesus meant one who would be like Him. And the word "counselor" means someone who acts as our advocate, giving guidance and coming alongside us to help.

Remember, this counselor, who is on our side and who is God, lives within us. "For he lives with you and *will be in you*," Jesus said, foretelling the Spirit's coming (John 14:17, emphasis added). We can't be any more connected than that! As a man, Jesus was limited in how He could relate to His followers by the physical body He occupied during His time on earth. But the Spirit has no such limitation. That's why Jesus said, "It is for your good that I am going away. Unless I go away, the Counselor will not come to you; but if I go, I will send him to you" (John 16:7).

When this counselor takes up residence in our lives, and when we cooperate with His work in our hearts and minds, He can start to produce His fruit in us. That's what happened when my life was changed so radically after my conversion. And when Earl and Sally rebuilt their relationship, making it stronger than ever, that, too, was the work of the Spirit.

So why don't we see more Christian marriages that have the quality and depth of Earl and Sally's? The reason is simply that we have failed to cultivate our relationship with the Holy Spirit. We won't look to Him for guidance and power until we practice His ongoing presence in our lives. But when we do, He will reproduce the love of Jesus in each of us and in our marriages.

To cultivate the relationship, we need to know the Spirit better and open more of our lives to Him. That's why we're glad you're reading this book—it will help you in that process. In the next chapter, we'll look more closely at how the Holy Spirit wants to give us guidance and direction.

Heavenly Father,

Before He returned to heaven, Your Son promised that You would send the Holy Spirit, that we would know Him, and that He would live in us. I pray that You will make me more sensitive to the Spirit's ongoing presence in my life. Remind me that He is always there and ready to help me. Impress upon my heart the ways that I grieve or disappoint the Holy Spirit.

Show me how I can relate to the Holy Spirit as a real person even though I cannot see Him. Give me the faith to depend upon Him as He teaches me about the Savior and seeks to reproduce the Savior's life in me.

I ask these things in Jesus' name. Amen.

5

How the Holy Spirit Leads and Guides Us

Robin, a pastor's wife, had dropped out of college as a young woman to help her husband get through seminary. Now nearing middle age, with her children mostly grown, she decided to return to school and finish her degree. Though her relationship with her husband, Ben, wasn't as close as she would have liked, he fully supported her in this decision.

In her first semester back at college, Robin took a sociology course. During the early lectures, she often found herself sitting near an attractive, friendly man who appeared to be about her age. After a few classes, they struck up a conversation. He told her his name was Frank, and he, too, was married. Before long, they were talking not only before and after lectures, but also later at a campus coffee shop.

Robin found herself increasingly attracted to Frank, especially when she learned he was also a Christian. More and more, she looked forward to seeing him and spending time with him. He made it clear that he felt the same. Somehow, she never got around to mentioning Frank to Ben.

After a few months, Robin and Frank were seriously involved emotionally. Though nothing physical had happened yet, they both knew they were falling in love. And since they were enjoying each other's company much more than they were their spouses' and were feeling much more compatible with each other, they came to believe they were meant to be together.

Robin, however, as a pastor's wife, didn't want to divorce Ben and possibly ruin his ministry. Nor did Frank want to hurt his wife's feelings. So they decided that the thing to do was to pray that their spouses would die so they could get married with a clean conscience. And that's exactly what they began to do.

As strange as that may sound, it's a true story (except for the names), and it's an example of how off-track our thinking can get even when we believe we're seeking and following God's will. It's safe to say the Holy Spirit was *not* leading Robin and Frank to pray that way—nor would He honor their request.

From the Spirit?

How can we be so sure the Spirit was not in their desires and actions? After all, we've heard many Christians assert that God was leading them in directions we personally wouldn't choose. Who's to say which interpretation of the Spirit's guidance is valid and which isn't? *The key test of whether any message or leading is from the Spirit is this: Is it consistent with the teaching of the Bible?*

If it's not, it's safe to say that the leading is not of the Holy Spirit. After all, the Bible is God's book. The men who wrote it were directly inspired by the Spirit in what they penned. "All Scripture is God-breathed and is useful for teaching, rebuking, correcting and training in righteousness" (2 Timothy 3:16). The Bible gets even more specific about its origin in 2 Peter 1:21: "For prophecy [for example, the Word of God] never had its origin in the will of man, but men spoke from God as they were carried along by the Holy Spirit."

Because that's true, because the Bible is God's truth for the human race, Scripture is the primary method by which the Spirit leads us. He wants us to obey His Word, not contradict it. If we refuse to obey we will not walk in the power of the Holy Spirit.

Returning to the case of Robin and Frank, the Bible clearly says, as we've seen in previous chapters, that we're to love our spouses sacrificially, with their best interest as our highest desire for them. Is that the way Robin and Frank were loving their spouses? Obviously not. In fact, Frank was violating the commandment that says, "You shall not covet your neighbor's wife" (Exodus 20:17).

Each time we take a step or make a choice, we want to be sensitive and responsive to the Holy Spirit's desires.

This matter of properly discerning the Spirit's leading is vitally important, as Romans 8:13,14 makes clear: "For if you live according to the sinful nature, you will die; but if by the Spirit you put to death the misdeeds of the body, you will live, because *those who are led by the Spirit of God are sons of God*" (emphasis added). In other words, the leading of the Spirit is a mark of a true believer, and He directs us to live to the glory of Jesus Christ.

Just how involved does the Holy Spirit want to be in our lives? Is His leading moment by moment, or is He only concerned with our big decisions? Several passages of Scripture give us insight. Galatians 5:25 says, "Since we live by the Spirit, let us keep in step with the Spirit." Each time we take a step or make a choice, we want to be sensitive and responsive to the Holy Spirit's desires.

Ephesians 6:18 tells us, "Pray in the Spirit on all occasions with all kinds of prayers and requests." In a similar vein, 1 Thessalonians 5:16-18 says, "Be joyful always; pray continually; give thanks in all circumstances, for this is God's will for you in Christ Jesus."

All these verses suggest the Spirit's leading is to be intimate and constant. But keep in mind that He is primarily concerned with our relationships with God and other people. We shouldn't go to extremes and ask Him what we should have for breakfast or what brand of jogging shoes to buy. However, when we're cultivating our love for the Savior and learning about Him from the Bible, the Holy Spirit wants to be involved. When we're talking with an unsaved neighbor, He may well encourage us to present the gospel. When we interact with our spouses, He wants to guide and empower, giving us marriages marked by the love of Jesus and the fruit of the Spirit.

When you can't understand your partner, pray for the Spirit's leading. When you've been hurt or frustrated by your spouse, pray again. And when you're having a disagreement with your mate, by all means pray, and be ready to obey the Holy Spirit's direction.

Discover What the Spirit Is Saying

How will His leading come? Primarily in two ways. The first is the Bible, which, as we've already seen, He authored. It's God's love letter to us, as well as His instruction book for our lives. He expects us to know it, and most of it is very straightforward and easy to understand. The Spirit has also gifted people to help us comprehend and apply His Word in our everyday experience.

Perhaps you, like us, have occasionally had times when you heard a sermon, a radio broadcast, a song, a testimony, a reading from the Bible, or you read an article or a book and thought, *That's speaking directly to me! How did that person know what I've been through this week?* When that happens, it's usually the Spirit speaking to us loud and clear.

Here are some things you can be sure the Holy Spirit is saying to you, because they come straight from the Bible.

To you as a couple:

- Be submissive to each other (see Ephesians 5:21).

- Honor each other in love (see Romans 12:10).

- Be kind and considerate of each other (see Ephesians 4:32).

To the Christian husband, He says:

- Be considerate as you live with your wife (see 1 Peter 3:7).
- Love her as Jesus loves the church (see Ephesians 5:25).
- Give yourself up for her (see Ephesians 5:28).

To the Christian wife, He says:

- Adorn yourself with a gentle spirit (see 1 Peter 3:4).
- Respect your husband (see Ephesians 5:33).
- Encourage your husband's leadership in the family (see Ephesians 5:22).

The second way the Holy Spirit leads us is by speaking directly to our minds and hearts. This is when we get a profound impression from beyond ourselves that we know we ought to do something. Sometimes this sense of leading is stronger than at other times, but again, if it's from the Spirit of God, it will *always* be consistent with God's written Word.

Let us give you an example of this kind of leading. Bill McCartney, the former Colorado University football coach and the founder of Promise Keepers, tells the story in the Promise Keepers' book *Go the Distance*. One Sunday morning, he was sitting in church with his wife, Lyndi, when a guest speaker made a pointed observation: "Do you really want to know about a man's character? Then look into the face of his wife. Whatever he has invested in her or withheld from her will be reflected in her countenance."

Now, up to that point, McCartney had thought he was doing a good job as a husband. He had even used his marriage as an example for the men at Promise Keepers conferences. But that morning when he heard those words and looked into Lyndi's face, he knew the truth. For years, he says, he had been pursuing his own dreams at her expense, taking her support for granted and not asking what was best for her. In response to that prompting from the Spirit, McCartney resolved to make a major life change (he resigned his coaching position shortly thereafter) in order to concentrate on better meeting Lyndi's needs.

How can we be confident that the prompting McCartney received that morning was from the Holy Spirit? Let's put it to the biblical test. Was it self-sacrificing? Was it honoring to his wife? Did it show her Christlike love? Was it considerate of her feelings and needs? Yes. He was acting on those things God requires of husbands in His Word.

⚬∞⚬

As a wife, I want to encourage husbands to do what Bill McCartney did in response to the leading of the Holy Spirit. I have seen John respond in similar ways, and it has given me constant reassurance that the Lord is working in our lives. We will fail each other, sometimes daily, but if we are willing to always come back and respond to the Holy Spirit, He can restore health to our relationship. Although my security is in the Lord, I find a great deal of comfort when it is obvious my husband wants to do the will of God.

⌇

Although it's not as clear-cut, the Spirit also leads us through the circumstances of our lives. Nothing comes our way that doesn't first pass through His sovereign protection. In the book of Acts, we repeatedly see where doors were opened and closed for the preaching of the gospel (see, for example, Acts 16:6,7).

But in our practical experience, does a closed door mean we should turn and go another way, or does it mean we should work and pray more to push it open? That's why circumstances alone are often not clear enough to reveal God's will. We also need to study Scripture and listen for the Holy Spirit's voice in our hearts and minds.

Finally, the Spirit may give direction through the counsel of others. Those people who know the Bible and understand what it means to be led by the Spirit can help us determine what He is saying to us. Praying and reading Scripture with such people can be an incredible way to connect with the Counselor.

⌇

It has meant a great deal to me that John has always trusted in my sense of the Spirit's guidance as we have sought to make decisions under His leadership. It has challenged me to pursue the Holy Spirit's direction in my life as I realize my responsibility in our spiritual partnership.

What's Your Response?

In this chapter, we've seen the major ways the Holy Spirit guides us into marriages that are centered on Jesus Christ and glorifying to Him. The question now is how will you respond? Here are some questions to get you started:

- Will you study the Bible in order to know what the Holy Spirit has said?
- Will you listen for the Spirit's guidance so you can have a Christ-centered marriage?
- Will you do what the Spirit tells you?

Once you commit to knowing and doing God's will, you'll find yourself in the middle of a spiritual battle. And you can't win this battle for your marriage on your own. You can only do it with the strength of the indwelling Holy Spirit.

Heavenly Father,

You have made it clear that those who are Your children are to be led by the Holy Spirit. I want to be led by the Spirit, so that in my life and in my marriage I will do what You want me to do and be what You want me to be.

Father, please use Your Holy Word to instruct me, guide me, and protect me from being misled or deceived.

May the Scriptures be a lamp unto my feet and a light unto my path. Also, Father, make me more sensitive to the inner voice of the Spirit as He seeks to lead me.

I pray that the Holy Spirit will lead us as a couple into a wonderful experience of loving Jesus Christ and one another.

In Jesus' name I pray. Amen.

6

How the Spirit Empowers Us

Bill and Susan had weathered almost 20 years of marriage. They had three children and were faithful attendees of a local Bible church.

There had been a number of traumatic events in their lives. Their middle child had been born with a congenital birth defect, requiring regular medical attention and a series of surgeries during her first few years of life. Bill had ventured into several different businesses, coming up on the short end each time. Finally, Bill and Susan were forced into bankruptcy.

Under the incredible financial and emotional pressures, Bill started to drink heavily. Before long it was obvious that Bill had become an alcoholic.

As their lives went from bad to worse, Susan never wavered. She continued to love Bill despite his many shortcomings. She didn't approve of his drinking, but she stayed with him, knowing that God wanted to do a special work in Bill's life and in their family.

Susan didn't grow bitter even when she had no choice but to return to her work in a local bank. Despite her emotional and physical fatigue, she spent most of her nights trying to reassure her children that their dad would be all right.

When Susan sought my counsel, I knew she was being sustained by the power of God. I was utterly amazed at how she was able to love Bill even when his actions made him very unlovable. Rather than focus on his failures and how they had negatively impacted her, she saw his alcoholism as the symptom of an underlying spiritual problem. Eventually Bill came to realize that the same power sustaining Susan was also available to him in his battle with alcohol, and now he is experiencing growing freedom from its threat.

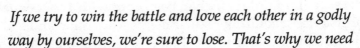

If we try to win the battle and love each other in a godly way by ourselves, we're sure to lose. That's why we need the power of the indwelling Holy Spirit.

If we're serious about cooperating with the Spirit to develop a marriage that honors God, we'll quickly find ourselves in a spiritual battle. Who are the enemies who will come against us? The answer is spelled out in two passages of Scripture.

First John 2:15-17 says, "Do not love the world or anything in the world. If anyone loves the world, the love of the Father is not in him. For everything in the world—the cravings of sinful man, the lust of his eyes and the boasting of what he has and does—comes not from the Father but from the world." Ephesians 6:12 says, "For our struggle is not against flesh and blood, but against the rulers, against the authorities, against the powers of this dark world and against the spiritual forces of evil in the heavenly realms."

We'll talk more about these enemies—the world, the sinful flesh, and the devil—in chapter 8. For now, I want to make it clear that we can't overcome them on our own. They're too strong for us. *If we try to win the battle and love each other in a godly way by ourselves, we're sure to lose.* That's why we need the power of the indwelling Holy Spirit. He, in and through us, can overcome these enemies and help us love each other as we should.

Navigating the Raging Currents

Loving our spouses in a way that honors God is what's best for us, both individually and in our marriages. But it's also important to God for a couple of other reasons.

First, it's a matter of simple obedience to His highest calling for all of us:

> Jesus replied: "Love the Lord your God with all your heart and with all your soul and with all your mind." This is the first and greatest commandment. And the second is like it: "Love your neighbor as yourself" (Matthew 22:37-39).

So we enter into this love relationship with God first and foremost, and that in turn is the foundation on which we develop our love for others. And who is a closer "neighbor" than our spouse?

Second, by loving our mates in a God-honoring way, we show the people around us that we belong to Him. We also model for them the love God has for them, too. Jesus said in John 13:34,35:

> A new command I give you: Love one another. As I have loved you, so you must love one another. By this all men will know that you are my disciples, if you love one another.

We are to love each other "as I have loved you"—the kind of love described in 1 Corinthians 13, the kind of love that is the fruit of the Spirit working in us. And when we do, all men will know that we are Jesus' disciples. And then they'll want to experience that same love in their own lives.

Let's make this really practical. I am to love Teri the way Jesus Christ loves Teri. If I do, the non-Christian people around us will be drawn to that love and want it for themselves. They may even ask us how we manage to love each other so well. But there's a problem. So often, we're tempted to be impatient, unkind, and inconsiderate with each other. And more often than we like to admit, that's the way we treat each other.

Why is that? Quite simply, we fail when we try to love each other out of our own resources—our own feelings and strength. When we succeed, it's because we're following the Spirit's leading and drawing on His power.

Imagine yourself in a raft in the middle of the raging waters of one of Colorado's awesome rivers. It's mid-May, and the heavy winter snow has melted, causing the river to run with tremendous volume and force. You hang on tightly as you hurl through the thundering rapids, dodging the floating logs and jutting rocks. If you're thrown overboard, the danger will be multiplied a hundredfold. You don't even begin to have the strength you'd need to battle the current and swim to safety.

Well, the combined force of the world's ways, the flesh within, and Satan's evil angels is like that raging whitewater. Taking advantage of your fatigue, pain, frustration, and disappointment, they want to drag you into the undercurrent of marital problems. Before you know it, you can find your marriage crashing into the rocks. And on your own, you don't begin to have the strength necessary to avoid them.

Spiritually speaking, the Christian life is one that runs upstream against the current of its enemies. The ability to succeed is supernatural. It's possible only with God's help through the indwelling presence of the Holy Spirit. He connects us to the life of Jesus, so that we can abide in Him, grow more like Him, and see spiritual fruit produced in our lives and marriages.

The Bible provides many examples of people to whom the Spirit gave the power for living above and beyond the normal course of life. The 70 elders who assisted Moses in judging the nation of Israel needed the Spirit so they could help carry the burdens of the people (see Numbers 11:16,17). Samson had superhuman power from the Spirit to carry out God's judgments until he broke his Nazarite vow (see Judges 14:5,6). King David's reign, the most remarkable in Israel's history, was marked by the special presence of the Spirit (see Isaiah 11:1-4). When Zerubbabel set out to rebuild the temple, he, too, needed the Spirit's power (see Zechariah 4:1-6).

Those are Old Testament illustrations of the Holy Spirit "coming upon" someone for a specific purpose. In the New Testament age, every believer has the Spirit living within, as we've already discussed. Just before the resurrected Jesus ascended into heaven, He told His disciples, "But you will receive power when the Holy Spirit comes on you; and you will be my witnesses in Jerusalem, and in all Judea and Samaria, and to the ends of the earth" (Acts 1:8).

Life-Changing Power

The word Jesus used for power is "dunamis," from which we get the word dynamite. However, Jesus was speaking not of explosive power but of a dynamic, emboldening, life-changing power that would come as a result of being indwelled by His Spirit. And that's the power that's in us, ready to help us "swim against the current" and live for Him. We must not allow extreme positions on the Holy Spirit to stand in the way of pursuing His power to live and love like Jesus.

Just where do we experience this power? The answer is found in Ephesians 3:16-21:

> I pray that out of his glorious riches he may strengthen you with power through his Spirit *in your inner being*, so that Christ may dwell in your hearts through faith. And I pray that you, being rooted and established in love, may have power,

together with all the saints, to grasp how wide and long and high and deep is the love of Christ, and to know this love that surpasses knowledge—that you may be filled to the measure of all the fullness of God. Now to him who is able to do immeasurably more than all we ask or imagine, *according to his power that is at work within us,* to him be glory in the church and in Christ Jesus throughout all generations, for ever and ever! Amen (emphasis added).

The Spirit works within us—in our minds, our hearts, and our will. It produces a deeper understanding of the love of Jesus, as well as the *ability* to love Him and others. This is consistent with the fundamental truth that when God gives us a command, He also provides the means—the power—to accomplish it.

Susan's ability to love Bill through many episodes of alcoholism was a product of her own experience of the depths of Christ's love for her. She was full of the love of Jesus, and it flowed from her heart to every member of her home.

When we experience this same love and power, it changes our lives and our marriages.

Father in heaven,

I confess that I have tried to live the Christian life my own way and in my own power.

Forgive me for my pride and arrogance, and show me how much I need You and the ministry of the Spirit in my life.

I want my marriage to be a demonstration of Your love. I know that the only way I can love _____ (spouse) the way You love us is through Your Holy Spirit.

Teach me what it means to rely on the Holy Spirit to love _____ (spouse) unconditionally and supernaturally with the very love of Christ.

In Christ's name I pray. Amen.

7

How the Holy Spirit Makes the Difference

Here's a typical scene in the Nieder household. From talking to a lot of people over the years, I suspect many of you will be able to relate to our experience.

I have had a particularly tough day at work. Perhaps we were recording some upcoming broadcasts in the studio, and things just weren't going right. We repeatedly had to stop and start over. Our guest was, shall we say, less than exciting. All that put me in a bit of a sour mood.

Then I went back to my office, and perhaps my secretary handed me the latest ministry financial report. "It doesn't look good," she said. It was summertime, and giving was way down. *I might have to make some tough decisions about cutbacks in the next few weeks,* I told myself, frowning.

As if those things weren't enough, let's say that I then received a call from a station manager. He tried to be very encouraging, but the bottom line was: "Yesterday's program just missed the mark, John. I really think you emphasized the wrong aspect of the issue, and you completely ignored the most important part." Hearing such opinions is never fun. Realizing he was probably right made me feel even worse.

Finally, after all that, I go home. I'm beat, beat up, and ready to collapse. I'm in what I call my semizombie state. The last thing I want to do is deal with more problems.

Wouldn't you know, though, Teri has had a few itty bitty problems of her own during the day. Things like a broken kitchen faucet that wants to do a good imitation of Old Faithful if you turn it on. Oh, and Erik "found" a "souvenir" the neighbor's dog left in our backyard again. Somebody really needs to talk to him—the neighbor, not the dog—again.

Teri has reached the end of her daily allotment of rope. Fearing she can't hold on much longer, she hands the rope over to me. Now, how am I going to respond?

There really isn't any time, day or night, when we can afford to be on our own, spiritually speaking.

I'm going to react in one of two ways. I will either ignore her plight, which is the desire of my sinful flesh and the choice I've made all too often in the past, or I will respond patiently, treating Teri with kindness and consideration in spite of my less-than-loving feelings at the moment. Patience is what the Holy Spirit desires for me. And because that choice would be so out of character for me, only He can make it happen.

That scenario illustrates the two basic kinds of situations in which the Holy Spirit can and must make a difference in our daily lives. First, we need to be sensitive to the Spirit's leading moment by moment throughout the day. That's because moment by moment the world, the flesh, and the enemy are seeking to mislead us and get us to act on our own rather than in the strength of the Spirit. That's why the apostle Paul said:

> So I say, *live by the Spirit,* and you will not gratify the desires of the sinful nature. For the sinful nature desires what is contrary to the Spirit, and the Spirit what is contrary to the sinful nature. They are in conflict with each other, so that you do not do what you want (Galatians 5:16,17, emphasis added).

As we've seen, all of us who have trusted in Jesus as Savior are indwelled by the Holy Spirit. Whether we recognize it or not, we have His constant presence with us. The phrase "live by the Spirit" tells us we need to stay in continual connection with Him. Then, a little further in the same passage, Paul said, "Since we live by the Spirit, let us keep in step with the Spirit" (Galatians 5:25). Here again, the idea is that we're to take each and every step with the Spirit rather than on our own. *There really isn't any time, day or night, when we can afford to be on our own, spiritually speaking.* When we're driving in the car, on the job, relaxing with the family, working in the yard, in the grocery store—at all times—we need to be in touch with the Spirit.

This sensitivity to the Spirit can begin at the start of each day, as we place ourselves on the altar, as it were, and give our day—control of our lives—to the Lord. "Therefore, I urge you, brothers, in view of God's mercy, to offer your bodies as living sacrifices, holy and pleasing to God—this is your spiritual act of worship" (Romans 12:1). And then throughout the day, we need to choose to stay in contact with and in submission to the Spirit.

Critical Moments

The second type of situation in which the Holy Spirit can and must make a difference in our daily lives is in what we call "critical moments." These are the times when we're dealing with people or difficult circumstances and we're strongly tempted to make wrong decisions. At times like this, only the Spirit's help will produce a Christlike response.

Now, back to our opening illustration about my day at the office. I faced critical moments when things went wrong in the studio (I could have gotten frustrated and angry), when I got the bad financial report (I could have despaired or doubted God's goodness), when the station manager called to criticize (I could have been defensive or bitter), and when I got home and Teri wanted some relief (I could have turned selfish or sharp-tongued). I might also have had critical moments when another driver cut me off in traffic or one of my children challenged my authority.

∽∞∾

I faced critical moments when the faucet erupted (I could have been angry at the faucet maker, John, or even God), when Erik came in covered with the dog's souvenir (I might have been tempted to kick the dog and/or its owner), and when John got home and didn't eagerly jump to my rescue as I thought he should (I might have given him a piece of my mind that I couldn't afford to lose!).

∽∞∾

In critical moments, the Holy Spirit wants to lead us and empower us to do the right thing. And we all respond in one of four ways:

1. We're out of touch with Him, and we don't have a clue to what He's saying.

2. We kind of know what we ought to do, but we think it's only our conscience speaking and not a big deal, so we ignore it.

3. We know exactly what we ought to do by the Holy Spirit's prompting, but we assert our will and refuse to cooperate.

4. We know what the Spirit wants of us, and we surrender to His will and His control and respond in a Christlike way.

Left on our own, we would make the wrong choice in most of our critical moments. But, fortunately for us, this is where another biblical truth comes into play. The Living Bible puts it well: "For God is at work within you, *helping you want to obey him,* and then helping you do what he wants" (Philippians 2:13, emphasis added). This is part of God's leading us by the Spirit, creating in us the desire to do the right thing and grow in Christlikeness.

Say Yes to the Spirit

Let's take a step-by-step look at how the Holy Spirit can make a difference in our lives in those critical moments. We'll go back once more to our opening illustration for an example.

First, before such a moment even comes, hopefully I have been walking in step with Him through the day, sensitive to His leading. The Holy Spirit has been at work in me, creating the desire to say yes to Him when it matters most. When I walk in the door at home at night, wanting to do nothing more than relax and recoup, and instead Teri wants to hand me what's left of her rope, I have to make a choice.

The world is telling me, "You deserve a break. Look out for number one!" My flesh is telling me, "You've had a tough day. Her concerns are trivial by comparison." And the enemy may be reinforcing those ideas by feeding me the thoughts, *Go ahead, jump all over her! She's not thinking of your legitimate needs, so why should you be kind and considerate to her?*

The Holy Spirit, on the other hand, is prompting me to recall God's Word—those passages that tell me to treat my wife with kindness and understanding; that tell me love is patient and not self-seeking; that tell me a harsh word stirs up anger. If one of the broadcasts I taped earlier that day dealt with how a husband can better meet his wife's needs, the Spirit may prompt, "Well, do you really believe what you were saying into a microphone just a few hours ago?" Or maybe I'll recall that Teri and I faced a similar situation just a few days ago, and that time I blew it, so this time the Spirit will prompt, "Here's your chance to do it right, to be more like Christ this time and give Teri hope that you're growing in this area."

So I choose to submit to the control of the Spirit. Galatians 5:16 calls this living by the Spirit. Ephesians 5:18 uses different terminology for essentially the same thing: "Do not get drunk on wine, which leads to debauchery. Instead, be filled with the Spirit." Just as wine can take control of our emotions and will, so we're to give the Spirit that kind of control. Just as wine can make us act unnaturally in a negative way, so the Spirit can cause us to act supernaturally in a positive way. Note, too, that in both verses just cited, we're told that submitting to the Spirit's control is what we should do, but there's also the implication that we can disobey if we choose. The Spirit, though He's always working to mold our will, won't overpower our choice. He won't force us to do the right thing—but He will help us to make the right choice.

Then, submitted to and filled with the Spirit, I can be patient and kind with Teri. I can set aside my desire to relax and, instead, meet her needs—talking gently with her, helping Erik get cleaned up, fixing the faucet (or at least calling the plumber), or whatever else she needs at that time. I can encourage rather than tear down. I can lighten her load rather than add to it. I can love her and give myself up for her, "just as Christ loved the church and gave himself up for her" (Ephesians 5:25).

The bottom line: We can be controlled by the world, our sinful flesh, and deceiving spirits, which leads to words and actions that will destroy a marriage and family. Or we can be filled with the Spirit, who can overcome those competing powers and produce Christlike words and acts in us. When that happens, Ephesians 5:19,20 says we will—

- speak to one another with psalms, hymns, and spiritual songs—sharing communication that exalts Jesus Christ

- sing and make music in our hearts to the Lord, revealing an inner joy which is part of the fruit of the Spirit

- be continually thankful to God the Father for everything—laying open our grateful hearts

Why is it, though, that so few Christians have lives which demonstrate that they are Spirit-filled? The sad reality is some of us don't want the Holy Spirit to control our lives. In some cases it is fear of the unknown. The idea of being controlled by a spirit disturbs us. But for most of us, it is not so much fear as it is rebellion. We have our own agenda, and we are more concerned about the things of the world than we are the will of the Spirit.

So can we ask you a couple of important questions? Do you want to be filled with the Holy Spirit? Will you allow the Spirit to control your life—especially as you relate to your mate?

We want to encourage you to say yes and begin trusting the Holy Spirit to make your marriage all that He intends, to the glory of Jesus Christ.

Dear heavenly Father,

Forgive me for those times when I respond in a sinful way to my mate or to the circumstances of life. Forgive me for simply reacting rather than depending on the Holy Spirit for a response that will honor You.

Father, help me not to be caught off-guard or out of step with the Spirit. Keep me alert for those occasions when I am especially vulnerable to the tug of sin, the ways of the world, and the flaming arrows of the evil one.

I choose to always be filled with the Holy Spirit to the glory of Jesus Christ.

In His name I pray. Amen.

8

Obstacles to
the Spirit's Work

Not long ago, I was speaking at a men's conference about the sin of lust and how we men have major struggles in this area. The fact is that most men are easily aroused by visual stimulation. For many, the temptation to move beyond admiration is strong. Mental adultery becomes commonplace. (See Matthew 5:27,28.)

My honesty about how men often have a problem in this area touched one man more deeply than I had expected. As I spoke, he began to cry uncontrollably. He sat in the audience with tears streaming down his face. At the end of my talk, when I opened the floor for the men to respond, this man stood to address us.

"Before today, I thought I was the only man who had this problem," he said. "I battle constantly with lust. You see, I'm a salesman, and whenever I travel, I can't resist the temptation to watch the adult pay-per-view channel in my hotel room."

Through tears of frustration and repentance, he went on to say how the in-room cable network provides a free preview of its seductive pornographic movies to entice men to buy the whole program. "I can't tell you how many times I've given in," he concluded sorrowfully. When he was done, because of his vulnerability, many other men also opened up and confessed their struggles with sexual temptation and sin.

I tell that story because it shows so clearly the three formidable obstacles to the Holy Spirit's work in our lives. They are the *world, sinful flesh,* and the *devil,* our spiritual enemy. Although we discussed these in chapter 6, now we want to look closer at how they work against us and how we can overcome them with the Spirit's aid. The primary scriptures we shared were:

> Do not love the world or anything in the world. If anyone loves the world, the love of the Father is not in him. For everything in the world—the cravings of sinful man, the lust of his eyes and the boasting of what he has and does—comes not from the Father but from the world. The world and its desires pass away, but the man who does the will of God lives forever (1 John 2:15-17).

> For our struggle is not against flesh and blood, but against the rulers, against the authorities, against the powers of this dark world and against the spiritual forces of evil in the heavenly realms (Ephesians 6:12).

In the case of that traveling salesman, his flesh had an appetite for the pleasures of pornography. It had perverted his normal, God-given, healthy desire for sex into something vile, and this appetite was insatiable.

The world—the dominant values and messages of our culture—worked hand-in-glove with his flesh to encourage him in that same direction. It told him, "It's okay to indulge your appetite. You've got needs, and watching porno films is a legitimate way to meet them. If it weren't, the hotel wouldn't offer them on its in-room network, would it?"

And the devil kept him a prisoner of his lust by deceiving him into thinking he was the only man who struggled that way. Thus, he felt he didn't dare admit his problem to anybody and seek help. He was afraid he would be condemned, so he continued to battle alone, and that was a battle he was sure to lose.

From that man's experience, you get an idea of how the three enemies of our soul work together to defeat us spiritually. But now let's look at each of them in more detail.

Well-Packaged Lies

Romans 12:2 tells us, "Do not conform any longer to the pattern of this world, but be transformed by the renewing of your mind. Then you will be able to test and approve what God's will is—his good, pleasing and perfect will." As we've said before, "the world" as it's used here is the dominant set of values and beliefs in our culture. It affects the way we think and, ultimately, the way we speak and act. The world's values are promoted through the media, both electronic and print, as well as in everyday conversation.

And what does our world tell us about marriage? It is something that's only as permanent as yesterday's newspaper. It's no longer a sacred union and a lifelong commitment. The statistics say you're not likely to stick together. That may have been the expectation in generations gone by, but we've been liberated from that! So, if you're not happy with your spouse, you owe it to yourself—you're entitled—to go out and find someone who will make you happier.

As far as the world is concerned, as soon as your marriage turns bad, it can be discarded like an empty soda can. Every day, we're bombarded with that message in ways subtle and not so subtle. It's a well-packaged lie that the world keeps pounding into our minds. We may not even realize it's affecting us until we begin to experience serious marital problems. And then the message takes on a power of its own. Suddenly, when we're emotionally spent, divorce looks like an attractive option.

⁓

Women need to be especially on the alert for the dramatic ways that our world is attempting to redefine our role and responsibility. Being a wife and mother is no longer viewed as an admirable way to invest one's life, yet the Scriptures refer to such a woman as being "noble" and worthy of special respect (Proverbs 31).

Tragically, more and more women are ready to leave their husbands and families in pursuit of what the world says is true happiness. Many who have bought into the world's offer are now finding it hollow, and they look back with profound regrets.

∞

Evil Desires

The flesh also seeks to influence us contrary to the will of the Spirit. In Galatians 5, the fruit the Spirit wants to produce in our lives is: "love, joy, peace, patience, kindness, goodness, faithfulness, gentleness and self-control" (verse 22). But Galatians 5 also lists the products of the flesh: "The acts of the sinful nature [better translated "the flesh"] are obvious: sexual immorality, impurity and debauchery; idolatry and witchcraft; hatred, discord, jealousy, fits of rage, selfish ambition, dissensions, factions and envy; drunkenness, orgies, and the like" (verses 19-21).

Look carefully at that last list. The next time you're tempted to be selfish, self-promoting, angry, jealous, envious, sexually impure, divisive, or one of the other sins named there, you won't have to wonder where that desire is coming from.

Make no mistake about it: Even though Christians have been given a new nature, we still have the principle of sin working in us, and its influence is powerful. Even so strong and mature a believer as the apostle Paul had to admit, "For what I do is not the good I want to do; no, the evil I do not want to do—this I keep on doing. . . . So then, I myself in my mind am a slave to God's law, but in the

sinful nature a slave to the law of sin" (Romans 7:19,25).
No wonder God said, "Sin is crouching at your door; it
desires to have [to control and eventually destroy] you,
but you must master it" (Genesis 4:7).

⊰∞⊱

*Although each of us has unique flesh patterns, it seems
we women are especially vulnerable to the tendency to want
to change our husbands and our circumstances. We think
that if we could just get our husband to respond or act in a
certain way, if he would just get a better-paying position at
work or show an interest in being involved at church, then
our life would be so much more enjoyable. Or maybe if we
could just live in a certain kind of house with a well-kept yard
and well-furnished interior, we would be happy. This is a control issue. We look for security in our husband, our family,
or our circumstances, attempting to control or change them
rather than acknowledge that our security must originate in
Jesus Christ and what He has done for us on the cross.*

*We also need to appropriate the cross in response to the
hurts we experience within our marriage relationship. Our
emotional makeup is such that it is much harder for us to get
beyond the pain of abuse and rejection and get on with our
lives. If we allow anger to establish a foothold in our hearts,
we soon become bitter, and our resentment becomes a wall
that few husbands can ever scale.*

⊰∞⊱

Satan's Fiery Darts

The third obstacle to the Spirit's work, the devil, is also powerful. The Bible tells us he is an angel, created by God to serve and worship Him. But the devil, also known as Satan or Lucifer, was filled with sinful pride: "You said in your heart, 'I will ascend to heaven; I will raise my throne above the stars of God; I will sit enthroned on the mount of assembly, on the utmost heights of the sacred mountain. I will ascend above the tops of the clouds; I will make myself like the Most High' " (Isaiah 14:13,14).

His objective was to take the place of God—the ultimate rebellion! And when God threw him out of heaven, he took a third of the heavenly host with him (see Revelation 12:4). We refer to them as demons or evil angels. Having lost his bid to supplant God, Satan seeks to destroy as many people as he can, condemning them to spend eternity with him in hell. The apostle Peter warned, "Be self-controlled and alert. Your enemy the devil prowls around like a roaring lion looking for someone to devour" (1 Peter 5:8).

How does Satan attack us? In Ephesians 6, when Paul was describing the Christian's spiritual armor, he urged us to "take up the shield of faith, with which you can extinguish all the flaming arrows of the evil one" (Ephesians 6:16). And what are these fiery darts (KJV) Satan shoots at us? From our study of Scripture, we believe that while his evil angels can't read our minds, they're very capable of placing thoughts there. They're students of our humanity—our weaknesses and our faults—and they use their superior intelligence and knowledge to attack us where we're most vulnerable.

More specifically, Satan's henchmen use deception. They plant lies in our minds and encourage us to believe them. Jesus said of the devil, "He was a murderer from the beginning, not holding to the truth, for there is no truth in him. When he lies, he speaks his native language, for he is a liar and the father of lies" (John 8:44).

In the case of the man who poured out his heart regarding pornography at the men's retreat, you can be sure that Satan had planted and encouraged him to believe the lies that pornography was all right, that watching it was a legitimate way to cater to his sexual drive, and that he was alone in his struggle with that area of life.

In the case of a married person in a troubled marriage, he or she might well be hearing thoughts from the enemy such as, "You deserve better"; "Divorce isn't really a big deal"; "He's not the man you married"; or "Nobody expects you to stay with a woman like that."

We need to be careful not to suspect Satan's presence around every corner, as some people on the fringe of Christianity are prone to do. However, we've also seen enough obvious demonic activity to know that the invisible spiritual war is real. Consider, for example, the case of Todd and Jennifer.

This Christian couple knew there was more to their problems than the world and the flesh. Jennifer had been abused as a child, and even though she went through years of counseling, she could find no freedom from her past. She was crippled by anxiety and had trouble maintaining her composure even in the midst of normal day-to-day activities. Todd was a caring and compassionate husband, yet Jennifer remained insecure and unable to relate, especially in the area of physical intimacy.

The Holy Spirit was ready and willing to be Jennifer's Counselor. Unfortunately, like many others we've seen, fear stood in the way of her allowing the Lord to do His work of grace in her life. Instead, she remained in spiritual bondage and eventually separated from both Todd and their children, saying she needed to start her life anew.

Clearly, the combined power of the world system, the flesh, and Satan's evil angels can be overwhelming. Their influence destroys marriages through adultery, verbal abuse, anger, discouragement, emotional abuse or abandonment, and the like.

What influence are these potent obstacles having on you and your marriage? Be honest with yourself. How do you overcome them? As we've said all along, you can't do it by yourself. You need the leading, filling, and empowering of the Holy Spirit. James 4:7 says, "Submit yourselves, then, to God. Resist the devil, and he will flee from you." First we submit to the Lord in the person of His indwelling Holy Spirit, admitting our need for and accepting His strength. *Then* we can successfully resist the devil.

Don't try to take on these opponents by yourself. For the sake of your marriage, do get—and stay—in step with the Spirit so that you can experience victory over the great enemies of a Christian marriage—the world, the flesh, and the devil. So if you are willing to have your life and marriage renewed by the Holy Spirit, acknowledge your need for Him and the importance of His ministry in your relationship.

Heavenly Father,

Please reveal to me the spiritual realities that I face as

I desire to live for You. Help me to understand the various ways the flesh affects me and my marriage. Show me any way that I have been taken in by the world and its ways. If there are any strongholds in my life or in our marriage, please make them known to me through the Holy Spirit.

Father, impress upon me that apart from the work of the Holy Spirit I cannot have victory over the flesh, the world, and the devil. I commit myself to depending completely on You so that I might walk in freedom.

In Jesus' name. Amen.

9

The Sting of Rejection

Sam and Joan were sitting in a restaurant, enjoying a delicious meal and pleasant conversation. Joan was feeling especially good because Sam hadn't asked her out on a "date" in a while, and it felt nice to be treated a little special again. Everything seemed to be going great.

Then another couple finished their meal, paid their bill, got up, and walked out. And with them went Joan's good feeling. Now, clearly visible on the other side of the empty table was a young, attractive couple in a booth. They were wrapped up in their own chatter and laughter, but Joan really wouldn't have noticed except for one thing—Sam was noticing them all too well. When Joan followed his intense gaze back to their booth, she looked a little closer and saw that the woman was attractive, and she was wearing a short, snugly fitting skirt.

Immediately Joan felt her cheeks turn red with shame and anger. Her first thought was, *How dare he?* But her second thought came just as quickly: *Well, why wouldn't he be drawn to her? I never was a model for looks, and I'm certainly not as slim or pretty as I was when we got married. Is it any wonder that he likes to look at a younger woman?*

Before long, Sam caught himself and turned his attention back to Joan. But she couldn't help noticing that he continued to steal glances at the other woman for the rest of their time in the restaurant. Joan felt a mixture of growing anger, insecurity, and rejection. Several times, as Sam turned his attention back to the younger woman, Joan started to say something, but she was too ashamed.

She finished her meal as quickly as she could, passing on dessert, to Sam's obvious disappointment. When she and Sam got up to leave, she felt only a sense of relief. She also noticed, as they walked out, that Sam looked back for one last glimpse of the young woman.

As they drove home, Joan thought, *Why does he always do this? No matter where we go, he picks out some good-looking younger woman and then can't keep his eyes off her the entire time we're there. He ruins it for me every time we go somewhere.*

Scenes and thoughts like this are all too common. Sam was being tugged at by the lust of the flesh. "The acts of the sinful nature," said the apostle Paul, "are obvious: sexual immorality, impurity and debauchery . . . " (Galatians 5:19). By indulging his interest in the younger woman, Sam was also being insensitive to his wife and her feelings.

Joan responded by getting angry at her husband. She felt his leering was not only insensitive toward her, but also a signal that he was rejecting her and found the younger, trimmer woman more interesting and more desirable. Joan strongly felt that she suffered by comparison . . . just like always. That, in turn, made her envy the young woman's looks and ability to attract men's attention.

Obviously, neither Sam nor Joan reacted well. Sam had an ongoing struggle with lust that he wasn't even trying to win. And Joan let his sin problem feed her feelings of rejection and inferiority, not to mention the anger that Satan is so eager to promote.

Confronting in Love

What difference would the Holy Spirit like to make in Sam and Joan's individual lives and in their marriage? What difference *could* He make? As we've seen in previous chapters, the Spirit wants to develop individuals and relationships that display the character of Christ. He works in various ways to do that, depending on our openness to Him.

If Sam is listening, the Holy Spirit might say to him, "May your fountain be blessed, and may you rejoice in the wife of your youth. . . . May you ever be captivated by her love" (Proverbs 5:18,19). The Spirit might also encourage him to think in terms of Psalm 19:14: "Let the words of my mouth and the *meditation of my heart* be acceptable in Your sight, O LORD, my strength and my redeemer" (NKJV, emphasis added).

The Spirit might hit Sam between the eyes with this verbal two-by-four from the mouth of Jesus: "I tell you that anyone who looks at a woman lustfully has already committed adultery with her in his heart" (Matthew 5:28). And we're confident that the Spirit would leaven His rebuke of Sam with an assurance like: "No temptation has seized you except what is common to man. And God is faithful; he will not let you be tempted beyond what you can bear. But when you are tempted, he will also provide a way out so that you can stand up under it" (1 Corinthians 10:13).

How will the Holy Spirit communicate these truths to Sam? If Sam has memorized these or similar verses, the Spirit will bring them to his mind at key points, at critical moments like the times when Sam first sees an attractive young woman and is tempted to dwell on the sight. Or Sam might hear the words in a sermon, a radio broadcast, or a statement made by a friend in a small group setting. He might read them in his Bible, a magazine article, or a book like this one.

When our children resist us, it saddens us. After all, we have their best interest at heart, don't we? So it is with the Holy Spirit. He is saddened when we do not do what we ought. If Sam keeps ignoring the Spirit's gentle prompting, the Holy Spirit may get his attention by letting him suffer the consequences of his wandering eye. Perhaps Joan will finally speak up and confront him. Perhaps other people may notice his habit and say something that Sam overhears. Or Sam might finally do something truly embarrassing while preoccupied with the sight of another woman.

When Sam is ready to get serious about honoring his wife and breaking his wandering-eye lust habit, the Spirit will be available and eager to help him find God's promised way out of temptation. Sam will have to make the choice to take it. This might include him getting into an accountability relationship with another guy or small group of men—"as iron sharpens iron, so one man sharpens another" (Proverbs 27:17).

Right about now, I can hear some men saying, "Wait a minute! We agree that it's wrong to desire women other than our wives. But maybe there's some reason for Sam's wandering eye. Maybe Joan hasn't been very responsive to his overtures lately, or maybe she's been sick and can't satisfy his desires. Doesn't that cut him some slack?"

In a word, *no.*

Naturally, there will be times when the state of the relationship, health issues, or other problems will cause a marriage to be less than satisfying for one or both partners—and it may even continue for a long time. That's certainly not the ideal, but neither is it an excuse to trample on a wife's feelings or violate God's ordinances. Also, the Bible's teaching doesn't change just because our circumstances might.

The bottom line on this issue takes us back to 1 Corinthians 13. The apostle Paul wrote, under the inspiration of the Holy Spirit, "Love is patient, love is kind. It does not envy. . . . It is not self-seeking" (verses 4,5). One paraphrase puts it like this: "Love cares more for others than for self. Love doesn't want what it doesn't have. Love . . . isn't always 'me first.' " That's the kind of love the Spirit wants to develop in Sam and in every husband.

The Solution for Rejection

And what about Joan? What does the Holy Spirit want to communicate to her? In the critical moments when she sees Sam looking at another woman and begins to feel rejected, the Spirit wants to come alongside and remind her, "The Spirit himself testifies with our spirit that we are God's children. Now if we are children, then we are heirs—heirs of God and co-heirs with Christ" (Romans 8:16,17). Furthermore, "He has made us accepted in the Beloved [Jesus]" (Ephesians 1:6, NKJV).

She is a child of God and a joint heir with Jesus, fully known and accepted by the Father. As such, her identity is secure where it matters most, and she is a person of great worth—regardless of what her husband does. To reinforce this crucial fact, the Spirit might also bring to her attention a truth like that found in Psalm 139:14: "I praise you because I am fearfully and wonderfully made; your works are wonderful, I know that full well."

In all the ways the Holy Spirit tries to prompt us and guide us, He is calling us to remember how much we are loved by God.

Regarding Joan's attitude toward Sam, the Spirit wants her to remember, "Love is patient, love is kind. . . . It is not easily angered, it keeps no record of wrongs. . . . [It] always trusts, always hopes, always perseveres" (1 Corinthians 13:4,5,7).

Rather than taking Sam's insensitivity as a statement about her identity, she needs to see it as his personal problem. The Spirit will prompt her to pray for him, certainly, and to love him and forgive him and do all she can to meet his legitimate needs. But the Spirit might also prompt her to confront him lovingly, explaining how his actions affect her.

∽∞∾

In all situations, in all the ways the Holy Spirit tries to prompt us and guide us, He is calling us to remember how much we are loved by God. He is calling us to be patient, kind, and honoring toward one another; to be sensitive to our spouse's needs and feelings; and to communicate honestly but lovingly at all times. He also calls us to exhibit a quality of love the world doesn't see nearly enough of, as we'll discover in the next chapter.

Dear Father in heaven,
   Thank You that You know me completely and You still love me. Thank You that I can come to You and know that I am accepted and never rejected.
   Help me, Father, to find my identity and security in You, and You alone. When I am rejected by others, including my spouse, may I find my comfort in You.
   With the help of the Holy Spirit, I will love and accept others as You have loved me. Reveal to my mind anything that I may have done that has caused _____ (spouse) to feel rejected. Show me how I can be more accepting of others—especially my mate.
   I ask this in the Savior's name. Amen.

10

"I Will Love You If..."

To others, Amy was absolutely charming. Her smile was warm and gracious. Her clothes were always impeccable. She was friendly and could make a new acquaintance feel instantly at ease. Your first impression was likely to be, "This is a nice person to be around."

Her interaction with Brian, her husband, was a different story. If you spent time with the two of them, it was soon obvious that, for some reason, she did not fully accept him. She often made derogatory remarks about his looks. When she was pregnant with their first child, she joked to coworkers, "The baby will probably be stuck with his daddy's banana beak of a nose!" On a number of occasions, with different people, she also commented, "On Brian's pitiful salary, I doubt we'll ever be able to do the things we really want, like buy a house."

In another situation, a man came to me one time and said his wife wanted a divorce.

"Why is that?" I asked.

"Because we can't afford to live in Forest Ridge," he said.

"No, tell me the truth," I insisted. "Why does she want a divorce?"

He repeated what he had said before, so I decided to meet with his wife.

"Why do you want to leave your husband?" I asked.

"Because," she said, "he doesn't make enough money for us to buy a home in Forest Ridge."

An incredible story, but true. In that case, like the preceding account of Amy and Brian, one spouse was giving the other only *conditional* love. "I'll love you *if* you measure up to a standard I've set," the spouse was saying.

Unfortunately, that kind of love is all too common in today's marriages. But that's what human love is like. It's self-centered, seeking the gratification of "my" needs and desires, and it's performance-based. This results in a lot of unhappy, insecure partnerships, and, ultimately, a lot of divorces.

In the case of Amy and Brian, her conditional love led him to feel he wasn't respected. She was violating the command of Ephesians 5:33: "The wife must respect her husband." In response, like so many men, Brian became driven to attain material success to satisfy his wife. But because he felt put down and inadequate, he also started to develop a deep and growing anger toward her, and that could only hurt the relationship in the long run.

Conditional, or human, love isn't totally wrong. It's reasonable for husbands and wives to have some expectations of each other. Conditional love can produce marriages that look very good—even better, in many cases, than the typical Christian marriage. But it's fragile, because it depends on continuing to meet the expectations of another.

Human love says, "I love you because you _____." It might be: "I love you because you're attractive, and that makes me feel more attractive"; "I love you because you're successful, which means I can be successful"; "I love you because you take care of me, which means I can feel secure." Whatever type of performance it demands, human love says, "As long as you give me what I want, I will love you."

Performance-Based Living

Without a word, many well-intentioned Christian wives put their husbands on a performance basis with the message, I will love you if . . .

- you pray with me
- you communicate with me
- you become more sensitive to me
- you start to meet my emotional needs
- you stop hurting me with your words
- you assume your share of the responsibilities in our home
- you make more money

The typical husband who's being loved that way won't say a word, but his spirit is being crushed. He feels rejected and incapable. Many Christian men feel inadequate in a variety of ways, but especially when it comes to their responsibility to give spiritual leadership in the home. They become intimidated when they try to communicate their own hopes, fears, and inner thoughts.

We suspect this lack of feeling accepted may well be the reason the men's movement has experienced such incredible growth—men long to admit their weaknesses and not feel rejected.

When the husband and wife meet each other's reasonable expectations, such as a sense of security or companionship, their relationship may well last a lifetime. But what happens when one spouse falls short in the other's eyes? First, the feelings begin to fade. Then disenchantment sets in, followed by frustration, and even anger. Before long, you hear one or both of them saying, "I don't love him" or "I don't love her."

The classic example of this is the middle-aged man who leaves his wife and children for the passionate embrace of his secretary. Why does he do it? For years, his love for his wife was based on what she gave him. He loved her because she was attractive, sexually exciting, and the mother of their children. But the years have gone by, and she's no longer the young beauty queen. Sex with her has become boring. The children have become more of a burden than a blessing.

With his young secretary, on the other hand, the man feels passion again, a sense of being young once more, freedom, and maybe even an acceptance his wife doesn't seem to offer any longer. And so this man says to the secretary, "I will love you (instead of my wife) because . . . "

Christians, too, are often guilty of demonstrating only a human quality of love. Christian husbands, for example, find it easy to apply the corporate "What have you done for me lately?" mentality to their marriages. Without a word, many of them communicate to their wives, I will love you if . . .

- you respond to me sexually
- you lose weight
- you keep the house in order
- you give me some space
- you stop nagging me about
  —being the spiritual leader
  —what's happening with the kids
  —fixing the back door
  —spending money on my hobbies

If we are to love people who are against us, how much more should we love and do good to our marriage partner?

Christian wives, in turn, may be crippled by insecurity and fear. They long for their husbands' love but never seem to measure up to their expectations. These wives become vulnerable to anger, bitterness, a deep sense of being a failure, and the flaming arrows of the evil one.

But relationships don't have to operate like this. In our marriage, even though I was verbally abusive and insensitive to her needs, Teri's unconditional love demonstrated to me the love of God and gave the Holy Spirit time to work in my life. It gave me time to change. During the troubled periods, she didn't withdraw her love. She didn't point a finger at me and say, "You, you, you—if only you..." (Well, maybe she did the "you, you, you" thing a couple of times!)

It almost goes without saying that the Holy Spirit wants to produce unconditional love in us and our marriages. Patient, kind, trusting, considerate, and selfless is the love God gives. This is the way He loves, which is no surprise since the Spirit's major goal is to help us grow in Christlike character and conduct. The Bible uses the Greek word *agape* for this quality of unconditional, fully accepting love. It's the kind of love God the Father has toward His beloved Son, toward people in general, and toward those who believe on the Lord Jesus (see John 17:26; 3:16; 14:21). (Imagine where we would be if God put us on a performance basis!) It's also the sort of love Jesus told us Christians should have for one another (see John 13:34,35).

Certainly, it's the type of love that husbands and wives should have for each other. To get a better idea of just how we should love each other, consider Jesus' words: "Love your enemies, do good to those who hate you, bless those who curse you, pray for those who mistreat you" (Luke 6:27,28). Now, if we are to love people who are against us, how much more should we love and do good to our marriage partner?

Let's make this very practical. We have found that when we become critical of each other, it works against the ministry of the Holy Spirit and plays to the schemes of the enemy. For example, at times in the past I have put

Teri on a performance basis regarding the shape of our house. I expected her to cater to my preferences. When she failed to perform to my standards, I got angry and let her know it. She in turn was hurt and tempted to strike back.

In that simple, common scene, spiritual warfare is taking place. The enemy of our souls is shooting his flaming arrows at me, wanting me to think, *You have a right to expect your idea of order! And you have a right—a duty, even—to let Teri know how she's not measuring up!* Satan wants me to feel proud and even righteous about attacking my wife!

He's also taking aim at Teri, encouraging her to think, *You're a failure! And because of that, John doesn't really love you. One of these times he may even get fed up and walk out on you!* He wants her to feel guilty, insecure, and afraid.

At the same time, the indwelling Holy Spirit is speaking to both of us. He's telling me, "Remember that love is patient and kind. Remember, too, that we're only talking about your preferences here. Calm down and let's focus on some of Teri's good points. Let Me help you love her the way you know you should—with My love." And in that critical moment, if I say yes to the Spirit, He will help me regain perspective, get control of my emotions, and love and accept Teri unconditionally.

∞

The Spirit is telling me, "Remember that love is patient and kind and not easily angered. Remember, too, that it takes two to escalate a situation like this. Calm down and let's focus on some of John's good points. Let Me help you love him the way you know you should—with My love." And in that critical moment, if I say yes to the Spirit, He will help me regain perspective, get control of my emotions, and love and accept John unconditionally.

⊸∞⊷

Perhaps that process sounds simple. We assure you, if you don't know already, it isn't. First, it requires that we stay sensitive to the Spirit's presence and leading. As we've said before, most Christians don't do that; so that alone is a new and challenging step. And the world, the flesh, and the devil will seek to distract us from that sensitivity at every turn of every day.

Second, it takes real humility to admit we need the Spirit's help to do the right thing. Again, the world, the flesh, and the devil want us to think we're basically good people who can and will do the right thing on our own. They don't want us to live in and be filled with the Spirit. And, of course, their ideas about what's right are very different from God's!

Finally, when we're being loved conditionally by our spouse, we have to decide that with the Spirit's help we are going to love unconditionally in return. Even with His leading and empowering, that can be a tough decision. When we make that decision, however, we're demonstrating true Christlikeness. And we're building a lasting foundation for the marriage relationship.

Heavenly Father,

If Your love for me was based on my actions, I would be in serious trouble. So often I fail to do what I know I ought to do, and yet You continue to love me.

Show me how I can love _____ (spouse) with Your kind of love. Free me from unreasonable expectations and a critical spirit. Constantly remind me that we are both works in progress.

In Jesus' name I pray. Amen.

11

Love Is As
Love Does

At the beginning of the preceding chapter, we told the story of Amy and Brian, using Amy's treatment of Brian as an illustration of some of the common forms of human, conditional love. Now let's look at their situation from Brian's side.

We mentioned that Amy's frequent put-downs were developing a deep anger in Brian. But before the anger came the pain he felt—the pain of feeling inadequate, rejected, ugly, and unworthy of her love. These feelings created the anger.

Unfortunately for Amy and Brian and their marriage, Brian chose to give back as good (or bad, actually) as he got. He would make self-deprecating jokes about his looks, especially his nose. But he also would inject an occasional comment about being broke because of Amy's wardrobe.

And he looked for opportunities to put her down for things she said and did.

As a result of this tit-for-tat trading of insults, their relationship went into a nonstop, downward spiral.

Now, what Brian needed to do (and the Holy Spirit wanted him to do) in his marriage wasn't easy. Brian needed to ignore his feelings and act in a loving manner toward Amy. This flies in the face of the philosophy that has prevailed in our culture for at least the last 30 years. And that's why we want to make a point of addressing it in this chapter.

Do the Right Thing

What has been one of the dominant messages of our culture in recent history? "If it feels good, do it." The popularity of that creed gave rise to the widespread acceptance of "recreational" drug use and premarital sex. How a person feels at the moment was elevated to the highest value. This mentality has invaded our entire society, including, for example, our schools, where pass-fail replaced letter grades in many classes, lest a bad grade hurt a student's feelings.

One implication of this philosophy that has been widely accepted is that if something *stops* feeling good, you have the freedom and the right to quit doing it. For instance, if your marriage stops feeling good, you no longer enjoy the relationship, and you conclude you're no longer in love, you're free to end it in a no-fault procedure. Never mind the vows you took on your wedding day about "till death do us part."

The net result of this mind-set is that people, non-Christian and Christian alike, tend to operate primarily on the basis of their feelings in all situations. But what the Holy Spirit says to us is that we need to choose to do the right thing—the Christlike thing—even when that conflicts with our feelings.

God is not telling us to have loving feelings.
He's telling us to act in a loving manner regardless of
how we feel. Divine love is a decision of the will.
It's what we do, not what we feel.

In Brian's case, he was feeling hurt, rejected, worthless, and unloved. He was also feeling angry and bitter. He felt that because Amy had created those negative feelings in him, he was justified in trying to get back at her. When he acted on that belief and got in a good verbal jab at her, he felt better, at least for a little while. He enjoyed it. But his entire response was motivated by feelings. He had no logic, no reason, and certainly no concern for or obedience to biblical standards or the leading of the Holy Spirit. The world, the flesh, and the devil were having a field day with him.

In our marriage, Teri's response most of the time was very different (for which I'll be eternally grateful). When I would get angry, she, like Brian, would feel hurt, rejected, and unloved. But she usually didn't let her feelings rule the day. She knew that sometimes, in order to do the right thing, she had to choose to ignore her feelings.

Let us take you back to Luke 6:27,28, where Jesus said, "Love your enemies, do good to those who hate you, bless those who curse you, pray for those who mistreat you." Is that something we're apt to *feel* like doing? No! Ninety-nine times out of 100, we feel like doing just the opposite: hating our enemies, doing bad to those who dislike us, cursing those who curse us, and condemning those who mistreat us.

But you see, in the Luke passage and everywhere else God commands us to love, He's not telling us to have loving feelings. He's telling us to *act in a loving manner regardless of how we feel.* Divine love is a decision of the will. It's what we *do*, not what we feel.

As we saw in chapter 10, this agape love reflects the character of God. It's how God the Father loves God the Son; it's how He loves us. To produce this quality of love in us is the Holy Spirit's major objective.

Note also that divine love is always given, never earned. We could never hope to earn the love and favor of a holy God; we could never be good enough to placate His wrath against our sin. Instead, His saving love is a gift freely given to us without merit on our part: "For it is by grace you have been saved, through faith—and this not from yourselves, it is the gift of God—not by works, so that no one can boast" (Ephesians 2:8).

In the same way, when we love like this (including our love for our spouse), we give our love away. We don't expect it to be earned, nor do we demand that our mate *try* to earn it. We love unconditionally. We love this way because we choose to do so. We make this choice even when our spouse has hurt us. We make this choice even when we don't feel like loving. What a contrast to the human love we usually see in marriages!

Making this choice, especially when we have to make it repeatedly because of numerous offenses—doing the right thing when our heart screams no—is one of the hardest things we can do. In fact, it's impossible to do on our own. Again, this is divine, supernatural love. It can come only when we cooperate with the divine Source, the indwelling Holy Spirit.

A Secure Love

One significant, positive good that comes from the decision to love this way is the incredible security it brings to the marriage relationship. When you know you're loved unconditionally, you tend to respond accordingly. Even if it goes against the anger that has built up in you over past hurts, even if it goes against your personality, and even if it takes a while to develop, you can't help but appreciate and warm up to such love from your spouse.

Many an abusive (verbal, physical, or both) husband has been won to the Lord by a patient wife who chose to love him divinely and let the Spirit produce that love in her. In our case, I was already a committed Christian, but Teri's unconditional love gradually melted my heart, convicted me of my sin, and helped me realize my need to change—with the Spirit's help.

Note, however, that loving divinely doesn't mean imitating a doormat. This love seeks the best interests of the one loved, and sometimes what that person needs most is a swift kick in the pants, so to speak. Once again, this is the way God loves us: " 'Do not make light of the Lord's discipline, and do not lose heart when he rebukes you, because the Lord disciplines those he loves, and he punishes everyone he accepts as a son.' . . . God disciplines us for our good, that we may share in his holiness" (Hebrews 12:5,6,10).

During those early years in our marriage, Teri needed to confront me over my verbal abuse for my own good as well as hers. She tried to do that several times, but I always blew up and then walked away. Only when things deteriorated to the point where we had a confrontation I couldn't avoid did I finally face up to my behavioral patterns and how they had to change. I needed to be confronted to face up to what I was doing wrong as a husband and father, and to change by submitting myself to the leading and empowering of the Holy Spirit.

How about you, especially in the context of your marriage? Are you ruled by your feelings, which come and go depending on the circumstances of the moment? Or are you choosing to love divinely, even when it goes against your feelings? Let the Spirit direct you. You can make the right choice knowing that He will help you to do what love does.

Father in heaven,
    You loved me even when I was Your enemy. And because You loved me, You did something. You sent Your Son.

Help me to get beyond mere feelings. Help me understand that love is a decision I make which demands I treat my partner as important and valuable. Show me how I can love, not simply with words but even more with my actions.

I will depend on the Holy Spirit for the capacity to act in love even in the most difficult times.

I ask this in the Savior's name. Amen.

12

But I Don't Want to Forgive!

At the end of a message I gave at a marriage conference, a dear man named Al came up to me with tears
streaming down his face.

"What's the matter?" I asked.

"Mr. Nieder," he sobbed, "last night my wife, Louise,
and I prayed together for the first time because of some
things we heard at this conference. I had thought things
were going well between us . . ."

He paused to collect himself before going on, and my
mind raced ahead to guess what he might say next.

Before my thoughts got too far, however, Al picked up
the story again. "Right after we got done praying, she
brought up something that had hurt her in the past. More
than five years before, I had told her in passing that I found
this woman employee of mine very attractive.

"That's all there was to it. Nothing ever happened between me and that woman. I don't know that she was even aware that I thought she was good-looking, because I never said anything to her. I didn't treat her any differently than my other employees. She hasn't even worked for me for several years now, and I've never seen her since she left."

"So as far as you knew, that was the end of the story, right?" I asked.

"Yes," he said, starting to cry again. "But apparently Louise has been stewing on that ever since. Last night as we talked, she was obviously bitter about 'the other woman.' I told her what I just told you—that the woman meant nothing to me, and there was never anything between us. But Louise just wouldn't listen. Now she won't even talk to me!"

Later, as I looked into the matter further, it became clear that Louise was, indeed, being unreasonable. She had latched on to Al's comment those five-plus years before and blown it all out of proportion. Ever since then she had let it fester in her soul, growing acutely bitter in the process. Al hadn't even known about it until the night before he came to see me. He had a genuine desire to cultivate a spiritual oneness with his wife, but she refused to close the door on the past and let him come close emotionally or spiritually. In the process, she was threatening to destroy her husband and her marriage.

Talk about your critical moments! The future of their marriage was on the line as they both considered what they could and should do in the days that followed.

⚭

Although it is easy for us to observe the situation as outsiders and conclude that Louise had obviously misinterpreted Al's comment, overreacted, and grown bitter, how many times have we been guilty of a similar response toward our spouse? Wives need to be particularly astute in this area. God has gifted us with sensitivity and perception that we are fully capable of misusing. I have seen far too many wives gradually enter into a mode of judging nearly every comment and action of their husbands in light of a prior offense. It is all too easy to grow bitter, critical, and overly sensitive. When the poor guy begins to feel like he can't do anything to please, he wonders, "Why even try?"

⚭

Even though Al hadn't really done anything wrong (though, in retrospect, he was probably unwise to mention the female employee's attractiveness to Louise at all), Louise had obviously taken offense. It was an issue for which she needed to forgive Al. What was the Holy Spirit saying to her? "Get rid of all bitterness, rage and anger.... Be kind and compassionate to one another, forgiving each other, just as in Christ God forgave you" (Ephesians 4:31,32).

Unfortunately, my marriage also provides numerous examples of the need to forgive—mostly of Teri's need to forgive me. For example, the deepest desire of her heart as a young wife was to become a mother. She had nurtured that longing since childhood. But to me, it was no big deal. I figured we'd have kids eventually, and that's about all I cared. Even when we struggled to conceive and Teri had to go through all kinds of difficult and embarrassing testing, I remained insensitive to the depth of her desire and pain.

To forgive someone opens the door to healing for us, for the person who hurt us, and for the relationship.

Extending forgiveness in such a situation is hard, to say the least. Our emotions naturally resist it. It may, in fact, be the very last thing we want to do when we've been badly hurt. However, the cost of not forgiving is too high. When we fail to forgive an offense and the offender, we grow bitter, like Al's wife, Louise. In casual conversations, we may look for ways to slander or gossip about the one who offended us. Malignant thoughts and harassing memories eventually distort how we look at life. We may even entertain desperate thoughts of revenge.

In short, we allow the memory and the pain to keep us in emotional and spiritual shackles. We're prisoners of the past, in chains of our own making. That's why forgiveness is in *our* best interest. It breaks those shackles and sets us free.

We also need to forgive because failure to do so interrupts our fellowship with God. Jesus said, "If you forgive men when they sin against you, your heavenly Father will also forgive you. But if you do not forgive men their sins, your Father will not forgive your sins" (Matthew 6:14,15).

This forgiveness from the Father is not the forgiveness we get when we trust in Jesus as Savior and receive the free gift of eternal life—that's a once-for-all-time forgiveness. Rather, Jesus was speaking in the context of our daily walk with God, our daily cleansing from Him as we confess our sins, and our daily forgiveness of others for their offenses against us.

In essence, Jesus was saying, "Don't come daily to me to confess your sins and be cleansed when you refuse to extend forgiveness to those who have offended you." The sin of unforgiveness indicates our hearts aren't right before God, which causes our fellowship with Him to suffer.

⤜⤏

What if Jesus were to respond to us with "I'm not ready to forgive that yet" or "It's too great an offense for me to deal with right now..."? How would we feel in the midst of this type of response? Yet I know I have been guilty of doing this to John, and I've seen other wives start down the road to destroying their marriages because they were "too hurt" to forgive the very one they've committed to love, honor, and cherish for life.

⤜⤏

Are you hanging on to some offense committed by your spouse, refusing to forgive him or her? If you are, you're cutting yourself off from the daily touch of God that can bring healing to your heart and hope and health to your marriage.

Open Your Heart

Forgiveness is clearly part and parcel of the love the Spirit is constantly working to develop in our lives. Furthermore, to forgive someone a great offense against us is to follow the example of our Savior, the Lord Jesus. When He, the only perfect and truly innocent man ever to live, was being nailed to the cruel cross for our sins, He prayed for His executioners: "Father, forgive them, for they do not know what they are doing" (Luke 23:34). If He could pray that way, then we, His followers, must learn to do the same. No matter what offenses we may have to endure, we will never suffer as unjustly as did He.

To forgive someone opens the door to healing for us, for the person who hurt us, and for the relationship. This means we can count on the world, the flesh, and the enemy to oppose any impulse we may have in that direction. That's why we can't rely on our emotions to tell us what to do when we've been hurt. Nor can we rely on our own strength even if we're willing to forgive. Forgiving is supernatural. It will happen only when we surrender our will to, and depend entirely on, the Holy Spirit.

Let God Be God

How will the Spirit lead us in this area? First, He will convict us of our need to forgive and the importance of not letting anger and bitterness take root and grow. Then He'll show us who we need to forgive and why. At least once a day in our private prayer times, it would be good to ask the Spirit to show us whom we still need to forgive. We should wait in silence for a minute for Him to bring to mind any people and incidents with which He wants us to deal. The Spirit will also assure our hearts and minds that if we turn an offense over to Him He will judge the offender in His own perfect way and time. We don't need to do His job for Him!

Finally, in those times when we're tempted to look for ways, both obvious and subtle, to retaliate against our offenders, the Spirit will remind us to return a blessing for a curse, and to submit to His control so we can say and do the right things.

The bottom line on forgiveness: God commands us to do it; it's for our own good; we can do it only with His help; and we need to do it even when our emotions scream that it's the last thing we want to do.

Does forgiving mean *forgetting* an offense? We'll take up this and more in the next three chapters.

Dear heavenly Father,

I know that I am to forgive others the way I have been forgiven through the cross of the Savior. I confess to You that I do not feel like forgiving those who hurt me.

Please show me by Your Holy Spirit anyone I need to forgive. Especially reveal to me any anger or bitterness I have toward _____ (spouse). By faith I am trusting in You to work in me so that I may forgive as I have been forgiven.

I ask these things in Jesus' name. Amen.

13

When You Are the Offender

I will never forget one particular time when I was giving a message in a church because, in the course of my sermon, I committed the preacher's cardinal sin. I told a joke on someone else that hurt the person's feelings. Making matters worse was the fact that the "someone else" in this case was my own dear wife, and she was sitting in the congregation.

Of course, before I told any joke involving her I should have asked her permission. Instead, however, I surprised her with it, and though I was obviously kidding, what I said was in bad taste. Afterward, when we discussed my message, Teri was visibly upset. "How could you tell a joke like that in a sermon?" she demanded to know. "You not only hurt my feelings, but you also embarrassed me in front of all those people!"

Did I, sensitive guy that I was, recognize and acknowledge the error of my ways, then follow that by offering a sincere apology? Well, no, not exactly. What I actually said was, "Come on, Teri, lighten up! It's not that big a deal! You're overreacting. Does the phrase 'making a mountain out of a mole hill' mean anything to you?"

Teri was not satisfied with that response. But for a while, I kept denying I had done anything wrong. I continued to accuse her of being too sensitive. I realize now that besides not taking Teri seriously during that period, I also wasn't listening to the Holy Spirit. Then one day not too long after that incident, the Spirit finally got through to me. He brought me under conviction by reminding me that it was Teri's sweet, sensitive spirit that had first attracted me to her. Yet here I was, trying to say that same sensitivity was the root of the trouble between us.

When I came to that realization, I was faced with a critical choice. Would I listen to my proud flesh and go on insisting I had done nothing wrong? Or would I submit to the Holy Spirit, admit my offense, and seek first God's and then Teri's forgiveness?

The Flip Side of Forgiveness

In the last chapter, we talked about the need to forgive those who offend us. But now we want to look at the flip side: how to respond when *we're* the offender. How to respond when *we've* been neglectful, abusive, insensitive, or have said or done something hurtful, or failed to keep a promise.

When we've hurt someone, we can be sure God wants us to make it right as soon as we can. Jesus gave us an idea

Our making amends with someone who has something against us is so significant to God that He even wants us to interrupt our worship of Him—the highest of human endeavors—in order to go do it!

of how important this is when He said, "Therefore, if you are offering your gift at the altar [that is, worshiping God] and there remember that your brother has something against you, leave your gift there in front of the altar. First go and be reconciled to your brother; then come and offer your gift" (Matthew 5:23,24).

In other words, our making amends with someone who has something against us is so significant to God that He even wants us to interrupt our worship of Him—the highest of human endeavors—in order to go do it! And if that's the way we're supposed to respond to any Christian, how much more so should it be with our husband or wife! We also read in 1 Peter 3:10,11, "Whoever would love life and see good days . . . must seek peace and pursue it." We're called to seek peace, to pursue reconciliation, and to live in harmony. Clearly, it's of great concern to God, and it should be for us as well.

But I Didn't Do Anything Wrong!

What happens if the offender doesn't think he or she has done anything wrong, even though the other person

thinks so? The principle of seeking peace and reconciliation prevails. With regard to that joke I told on Teri, for
example, even if I truly continued to think I had done
nothing wrong, she had clearly taken great offense. So I
should have gone to her and sincerely said, "Teri, I didn't
mean to hurt you. I didn't think that what I said would
do that. But I obviously misjudged, and my words hurt
you and embarrassed you, and for that I'm very sorry. Will
you please forgive me?"

What actually happened was that, as I mentioned earlier, the Holy Spirit brought me under clear conviction that
what I had said and done *was* wrong. Then I faced the
choice of whether I would continue to be proudly defiant
or submit to the Spirit and value the restoration of my
marriage over hanging on to my ego. When I say it that
way, the choice sounds simple, doesn't it? Who could make
a valid case for pride? But, of course, it wasn't really that
easy. My flesh was telling me, "You didn't really do anything so bad. She's the one who's blowing things all out
of proportion! Why should *you* apologize?" And the devil,
I suspect, was feeding me thoughts like, "She'll think less
of you if you say you were wrong. Real men don't ask for
forgiveness!"

I wrestled with these thoughts and feelings for a while
and, I'm happy to say, finally surrendered to the Spirit. I
apologized to Teri and asked for her forgiveness. She gra-
ciously forgave me.

Here are some guidelines for approaching your spouse
when you've been the offender:

1. Confess your sin and repent to God. Making things
   right with Him should be your top priority. "If we

confess our sins, he is faithful and just and will forgive us our sins and purify us from all unrighteousness" (1 John 1:9).

2. Before you approach your mate, commit the whole situation to God in prayer. Ask Him to work in your partner's heart, making him or her tender toward you and ready and willing to forgive. Ask Him to work in your own heart and mind, so that your motives will be right as you go, and so that you can be sincerely humble and loving.

3. Your side of the conversation with your spouse needs to include three elements: 1) "I was wrong, and I'm sorry." Even if you didn't think you were committing an offense at the time, you have to acknowledge that you caused pain for your mate and tell him or her you're sorry. 2) "I will do my best not to commit that offense again." This is repentance, a "turning away" from the wrong you've done. This is also proof of your sincerity. This says that you take what you did—and the pain it created—seriously enough that you don't want to do it again. 3) "Will you forgive me?" These are hard words to say because they put you at the mercy of your spouse. But they also open the door to reconciliation. They give him or her the opportunity to accept your apology and restore the relationship.

Now, back to our case. The Spirit did a good job of convicting me of how wrong I had been because I was sincere in my apology and repentance. In fact, I don't think I've said anything publicly that might hurt Teri since that episode. The Spirit has kept my heart and mind sensitive to that possibility.

But what if you go to your spouse with a sincere apology for some offense and ask for forgiveness, and he or she says, "No, I don't think I can do that yet" or "You've hurt me too much"? What then? Such a response is a definite possibility, and you need to be prepared for it—especially if your offense or the pain it caused was great. But it will be less of a crisis moment for you if you remember, going in, that love is patient, kind, and gentle. Ask the Holy Spirit to strengthen you in those areas before you go to your mate. Then, if you're not forgiven right away, you can do the following:

1. Say a brief prayer, again committing the situation to the Spirit and asking for His help, and tell your spouse that you understand and it's okay.

2. Repeat your determination not to repeat the offense.

3. Tell your mate you love him or her and appreciate his or her putting up with you.

4. Then wait and pray and stay in step with the Spirit so you can keep your promises.

And what happens if the offender doesn't approach you? The person who was offended has the responsibility to forgive even if the offender never asks for it, as we saw in the last chapter. Forgiveness is primarily between us and God, and we can forgive a person in our heart because God commands it and we know it's for our own good. For that to happen, we never even need to talk to the offender. But for the relationship between the two people to be reconciled, one of them has to take the initiative to approach the other, and the offender has to admit the offense and ask for forgiveness.

Remember: Forgiveness is an area where there isn't the slightest doubt about the Holy Spirit's leading, because it comes straight from God's Word. If you have hurt your spouse in any way, the Spirit wants you to confess it, repent of it, and seek your mate's forgiveness. And what the Spirit asks you to do, He will always empower you to fulfill.

Dear Father in heaven,

Through Your Spirit, please reveal to my mind the ways I have offended my mate so that I might seek forgiveness and with Your help restore our relationship.

Please help me deal with my pride and prepare _____(spouse's) heart.

In Jesus' name. Amen.

14

Do I Have to Forgive That *Again?*

When Barbara and Matt came to their first counseling session, I thought there might still be hope for them. I had Matt wait in the reception area while I brought Barbara into my office. As soon as I asked what their problem was, she began to cry uncontrollably. After what seemed like a long time, she finally blurted out, "I just want to be loved!"

After she regained some composure, Barbara tried to explain what had been going on in her marriage for more than 20 years. She kept referring to paper towels, and I struggled to understand what was so important about them. Finally she said, through her tears, "If I use more than one at a time, he screams at me." As she continued, I came to understand that if she or the kids used more than one paper towel to dry their hands, Matt would explode in rage. The same would happen if anyone left lights on in an unoccupied room. In fact, throughout their married life, Barbara had to account for every dime she spent, even though they lived in a huge home in an exclusive neighborhood.

In short, Matt had hurt, insulted, and offended her almost every day of their marriage—for more than 20 years by the time they came to me for counseling!

To make matters worse, Barbara had a distorted view of what it means to submit to her husband's leadership. As a result, she put up with his oppression for years without saying a word, even though she was screaming inside.

Then she met a man at work who was kind to her. He was just a friend; there was no hint of adultery. But the contrast between his treatment and Matt's was enough to push her into a decision—she wanted out of her marriage. Nothing I could say would change her mind. When I brought up anything like reconciliation, she would start to cry again and say, "I'm so old . . . I just want to be happy." As far as she was concerned, there was no turning back.

The irony, though it's common in such situations, is that when I met with Matt, he didn't have a clue that his marriage was probably over, that Barbara was essentially gone, already emotionally divorced. He wanted to make things right. He was even prepared to let her and the kids start using all the paper towels they wanted!

In most ways, with most people, Matt was a nice guy. People at church would say he was a solid Christian. But because of his own background, he always had that one terrible blind spot of being a fanatical cheapskate. Consequently, he offended Barbara over and over until she was finally at the breaking point.

We wives are to be responsive to the leadership of our husbands, but that does not mean that we avoid speaking the truth in love. Obviously, there are many times we should just overlook things—so many perceived offenses are the result of pettiness. But in Barbara's case, she never spoke up. Matt was not only hurting her, he was hurting himself and their marriage by following a path of sarcasm, criticism, and continual negativism. Barbara was not overlooking Matt's behavior but rather overloading her emotions with the offense, choosing to travel down a dark path of bitterness, journeying to what seemed to her to be the "point of no return."

When Is Enough Enough?

Unfortunately, through habits, pet peeves, and just plain insensitivity, husbands and wives have an incredible ability to irritate or hurt each other repeatedly. Forgiving these offenses—forgiving the *same* offense for what seems like the five-hundredth time—is one of the tougher challenges the Holy Spirit gives us. Nonetheless, that is His leading as we see clearly in Scripture.

You'll recall, for example, that 1 Corinthians 13:4 tells us love is patient. The word used here for *patient* means "to suffer long."

First Peter 4:8 says, "Above all, love each other deeply, because love covers over a multitude of sins." Notice that divine love, which is what Peter was referring to, *covers*

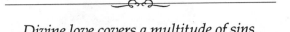

Divine love covers a multitude of sins.
That suggests not only a large quantity of offenses,
but also frequent repetition of the same ones.

the sins of others. It takes them out of view and out of consideration when we're dealing with those people. It covers sins the way a wet blanket covers a burning ember—extinguishing the flame and keeping a dangerous fire from developing.

Divine love covers a *multitude* of sins. That suggests not only a large quantity of offenses, but also frequent repetition of the same ones. If *the Spirit* is producing the fruit of His love in us, we'll have the capacity to truly forgive multiple offenses from our spouse. Remember how Peter came to Jesus and asked, " 'Lord, how many times shall I forgive my brother when he sins against me? Up to seven times?' Jesus answered, 'I tell you, not seven times, but seventy-seven times' " (Matthew 18:21,22). Peter thought he was being reasonable in proposing a seven-times forgiveness, which was beyond the standard taught by the religious leaders of his day.

Jesus, however, had a different standard in mind. In answering "seventy-seven times," He didn't mean we should literally count up to seventy-seven times in forgiving someone, and then on the seventy-eighth time say, "That's it! No more! You've maxed out your limit!" By greatly multiplying Peter's number, Jesus was actually indicating *there should be no end to forgiveness.*

That seems to be a hard, maybe impossibly high standard to meet. But let's look at that standard from three related points of view. First, put yourself in the place of the offender. Suppose you have some habit or practice that always bothers your spouse. You don't mean to give offense, but you haven't been able to break the habit. How many times do you want your mate to forgive you? Do you want him or her to stop at 77 times? We doubt it. *So forgive as you want to be forgiven.*

Second, ask yourself (and answer honestly) how many times God forgives you for the same offense. Perhaps you're repeatedly guilty of envy, jealousy, gossip, materialism, laziness, lust, or some other "pet" sin. If you're like most of us Christians, you're often guilty of ignoring the Holy Spirit's leading. And sometimes you try to empower yourself and live righteously—or at least acceptably—on your own. Whatever sins you've committed today or in the past, or will commit in the future, God has forgiven them all, no matter how many times you make the same poor choice. "As far as the east is from the west, so far has he removed our transgressions from us" (Psalm 103:12). *So forgive as you have been forgiven.*

Third, when you forgive someone over and over, who benefits the most from your decision? As we saw in chapter 12, *you* do. Refusal to forgive, even if it's the seventy-seventh time you have to do it or the seven hundredth, will lead to bitterness and anger in *your* spirit, while the person you're refusing to forgive may not even be aware there's a problem. If you refuse to forgive, then, you're the biggest loser. But if you make the tough choice to forgive, asking the Spirit to help you do it sincerely and completely, you're the biggest winner. *So forgive for your own sake.*

What Forgiveness Really Means

"How can I forgive when he hurts me again? Every time I look at him, or every time we're in the situation where he usually commits the offense, I'm reminded of what he's done in the past. All the painful feelings come to the surface again." If that's your response, we understand and sympathize. Yours is a tough position to be in, indeed.

Looking more closely at what it means to forgive might help you in this case. Our experience indicates, in fact, that most Christians don't really understand what's involved. So let's define it more clearly, beginning with several things forgiveness is *not*.

First, forgiveness does not mean condoning the offense. In order to forgive, you don't have to say that what the person did was okay. The words or actions probably weren't okay, and certainly the pain you feel isn't. You don't have to pretend that everything is fine when it really isn't. There's never a time when you have to fake it with God.

Second, forgiveness is not forgetting. Although the choice to forgive is a decision that's made at a specific point in time, the emotional and spiritual healing process—of which forgetting is a part—is usually gradual and requires more work. You will remember past offenses occasionally, especially if they were serious or repeated.

If that's your experience, you need to guard your decision to forgive by taking every thought captive in obedience to Christ. Whenever the forgiven offense comes to mind, immediately turn to the Spirit in prayer and say, "Please take this thought from my mind. I've already given this matter to You to judge as You deem best." Don't dwell on the offense for even a moment. Now, realize you may need to do this many times a day, especially right after the offense takes place. That's okay. As you turn the matter over to the Spirit, allowing Him to direct your thought life, your situation will get better even though it may take a while. Give yourself and the Spirit time to renew your mind in keeping with the Word of God.

And third, forgiveness doesn't necessarily mean that you have to see or even speak to the offender about it. Of course, if the person who hurt you is your spouse, you're going to see him or her. The point is that *forgiveness is primarily a matter between you and God.* God may, through the indwelling Spirit, direct you to lovingly confront the person and pursue reconciliation. Or He may not, depending on the nature of the offense and the effect it had on your relationship with the other person. And even if He does, it will only be after you've already forgiven the person in your heart.

Those are some things that forgiveness is not. So what, then, is it? Forgiveness is an obedient response to God's clear command to forgive those who have wronged us. It's a decision we make. Like love, it is not a feeling. In fact, it will often run counter to our feelings, which say things like "I want revenge!" or "Why should I have to forgive the same offense for the thousandth time?" Forgiveness is a sincere choice to release the person who hurt us from the obligation he or she incurred at the time. We also give up our "right" to retaliate or seek vengeance, allowing God to be the judge of the offender and what happened.

As noted earlier, once we make the decision to forgive, we have to guard it against the residual emotions that will urge us to pick up the offense again every time we remember it. *Just as we need the Holy Spirit's help when we decide to forgive, so we need His strength every time the offense comes to mind.*

The Sacred Act of Forgiving

A good test of whether we've actually forgiven someone is to look at how we think of the person who hurt us each time he or she comes to mind. At first, when the pain is fresh, there's likely to be lingering anger and bitterness. We need to take that to the Lord and ask for help for ourselves and a *blessing* for the other person. That may be hard and, again, contrary to what we're feeling at the time. But gradually our feelings should come into line so that we can say honestly, "I genuinely wish that person well." (Of course, all this will take longer if the offense continues to be repeated.)

Throughout Scripture, God gives us a number of word pictures to show us what He means by forgiveness. Here are three:

- To forgive is to turn the key, open the cell door, and let the prisoner walk free.
- To forgive is to grant a full pardon to a condemned criminal.
- To forgive is to throw an offense overboard and let it sink to the bottom of the ocean, never to be brought up again.

Finally, let us reiterate once more that forgiveness is a sacred and supernatural act of obedience to God. It is possible only with the guidance and assistance of the Holy Spirit. We do it because we've already been forgiven far more by God than we'll ever be hurt by any human offender.

Some common repeat offenses that need to be forgiven include:

- the failure to communicate
- not picking up around the house
- spending beyond your means, or not keeping good financial records
- general insensitivity to each other's needs
- less-than-receptive response to spouse's sexual desires

No doubt you could add to this list from your own experience. Throughout your day-to-day marital life, the Spirit is saying to you, "Don't major on the minor irritations of living together. Don't let your mind dwell on those things; instead, focus on what's positive about your spouse. And remember how you've been forgiven by God." Remember, too, that ongoing offenses will seem like a bigger deal when you're tired, out of touch with God, or emotionally vulnerable.

After all is said and done, the issue of forgiving repeated offenses boils down to this:

1. When an offense occurs for the first time, causing hurt, say yes to the Spirit and ask for His help to forgive.

2. When the offense occurs for the tenth time, causing anger and frustration, say yes to the Spirit and ask for His help to forgive.

3. When the offense occurs for the five-hundredth time, causing despair, say yes to the Spirit and ask for His help to forgive.

———————

Dear heavenly Father,

You have forgiven me for so much, and I am grateful. I have committed certain sins over and over again, and yet I know You continue to be merciful and gracious to me.

Father, help me to extend this same forgiveness even when _____ (spouse) does the same thing over and over again. By the power of the Spirit within, I am willing to forgive not just once or twice but even 70 times seven.

All for the glory of Jesus Christ, in whose name I pray. Amen.

15

The Anguish of Adultery

When Frank and Sally came to me for help, it was a last-ditch effort to save their marriage. Frank had been carrying on an adulterous affair for more than a year, and Sally now had proof that he couldn't deny.

"When I first knew for sure, the pain and embarrassment seemed unbearable," she told me. "I couldn't believe he'd done that to me—to us. I didn't *want* to believe it."

The more she thought about it, the more the pain grew. Soon it turned to anger. Before long she was thinking, *Our marriage is over. There's no way I can forgive this ultimate betrayal, and there's no way I can go on living with him.*

Not surprisingly, it was Frank who approached me first to see if there was any hope for their marriage. I sensed he was truly sorry and wanted to make things right with Sally. "But all my attempts have been brushed aside," he said. "She's so bitter and hostile."

Humanly speaking, Frank was getting exactly what he deserved. Humanly speaking, Sally was reacting pretty much as you'd expect. And those forces that seek to destroy marriage didn't help. "You shouldn't put up with that," the world told Sally. "You'll be happier if you walk away and start over with someone more trustworthy." Her flesh said, "This really hurts! What's the quickest and easiest way to stop this pain?" And Satan sent his flaming arrows that encouraged Sally to think, *You're not woman enough to keep him! And even if you were, you'd never be able to trust him again. Get out now! Don't even think of giving him another chance. Get even instead. Make him hurt the way he's hurt you!*

But what was the Holy Spirit saying to Sally in all this? "Get rid of all bitterness, rage and anger. . . . Be kind and compassionate to one another, forgiving each other, just as in Christ God forgave you" (Ephesians 4:31,32). In short, even though Frank had committed a horrible offense against her and a terrible sin against God, and even though it could be argued that Sally had biblical grounds for divorce (see Matthew 5:32), the Spirit's desire was that she begin to rebuild her marriage by forgiving Frank, just as she had been forgiven all her sins by God in Christ. Though it would take time for healing and restoration of trust, if Sally were willing, her marriage could become a trophy of grace, of the power of divine love over the power of sin. It was up to her and her response to the leading of the Holy Spirit.

Perhaps it would help Sally—and you, if you've been a victim of adultery—to realize that the Spirit is praying for you in your time of great pain. Read carefully and meditate on these wonderful words from the apostle Paul:

> In the same way, the Spirit helps us in our weakness. We do not know what we ought to pray for, but the Spirit himself intercedes for us with groans that words cannot express. And he who searches our hearts knows the mind of the Spirit, because the Spirit intercedes for the saints in accordance with God's will. And we know that in all things God works for the good of those who love him, who have been called according to his purpose (Romans 8:26-28).

Many times, as we have counseled people devastated by the infidelity of a spouse, we've seen those words— the incredible truth that the Spirit sees your pain, knows what you're going through, and is Himself praying for you to the Father—act as a healing salve on their wounded hearts. When we have experienced rejection and brokenness, the Holy Spirit can use it as fertile soil, planting Himself deeply within us to bring forth His fruit with great bounty. And we pray right now, even as we're writing these words, that you, too, will take supernatural comfort in the assurance that the Spirit is praying for you as well.

The Pain of Betrayal

If your husband or wife has committed adultery, forgiving him or her may be the hardest thing you ever have to do. But may we tell you, lovingly but firmly, that we believe the Holy Spirit of God wants you to know and act on these things:

First, God forgives adultery, and so can you. There's *no* sin that's not covered by God's forgiveness. His grace is that great.

Second, don't make any decisions until you've had time to pray and to stabilize emotionally. When you first learn of your spouse's infidelity, you're likely to be very emotional. That's *not* the time to make choices you'll have to live with for the rest of your life. Give yourself a cooling-off period. Believe us, it's in your own best interest.

Third, after you've cooled off, with the help and encouragement of some godly friends, respond biblically. Give your mate over to the Lord by an act of forgiveness. Let God be the judge of what happened. Ask Him to heal your heart and rebuild your love for your spouse. Also ask Him to do whatever work is needed in your mate's heart.

Fourth, determine to find your security in the Lord and not in anyone else. You're in a highly uncertain period. Perhaps, as mentioned earlier, your spouse's adultery has you questioning your own attractiveness and desirability. Maybe your mate is also making decisions you have no control over. Whatever you're facing, remember that you are a child of God. He loves you unconditionally, and nothing—"neither death nor life, neither angels nor demons, neither the present nor the future, nor any powers, neither height nor depth, nor anything else in all creation, will be able to separate us from the love of God that is in Christ Jesus our Lord" (Romans 8:38,39). Let your security rest in those unshakable facts.

Finally, as we said regarding repeat offenses, you need to take captive any disruptive thoughts and feelings. Don't let anger and bitterness take root in your mind, and don't let your thoughts dwell on images of your spouse with the other person. Instead, take all those thoughts to God, through the Spirit, and say simply, "Lord, help me! Replace these thoughts with Your comfort, Your truth, Your peace." Do it as often as necessary, day by day.

Critical moments will come for you when you're first deciding whether to extend forgiveness, when angry or bitter thoughts come to mind, and when you and your spouse try to reestablish physical intimacy. When those moments come, seek the Spirit and His leading. "Submit yourselves, then, to God. Resist the devil, and he will flee from you. Come near to God and he will come near to you" (James 4:7,8).

Let God come near to you. Resist the devil, the world, and your sinful flesh as they try to tear apart your marriage. Ask for and receive God's strength to do and say the right things. In time, as you're patient with yourself and your spouse, your relationship can not only survive but even thrive.

Now, back to the story of Sally and Frank. In counseling, I gave her some time to express her pain and sense of betrayal. Her feelings were genuine and legitimate. But long-term, I knew she needed to forgive Frank for her own well-being. When the time seemed right, I told her she needed to tell the Lord all she had been telling me.

She agreed and started to pour out her heart in prayer. I cried along with her. Then, with the Holy Spirit guiding her as her Counselor, she started to tell God how she felt about forgiving Frank. She was in a spiritual war between her emotions and her desire to trust God to be the judge of what had happened. She didn't want to surrender her longing to hurt Frank the way he had hurt her.

But then, no doubt prompted by the Spirit, Sally remembered the words of Romans 12:19: "Do not take revenge, my friends, but leave room for God's wrath, for it is written: 'It is mine to avenge; I will repay,' says the Lord." It was a sacred moment, and I was privileged to be there, because Sally then prayed, "Lord, I forgive Frank for being unfaithful. Please take this terrible pain away."

And in that moment, God began a healing work in her heart and in their marriage.

For the Adulterer

If you're the guilty party and you're still involved in adultery, the Spirit's message to you is simple and straightforward: *Stop the affair and get right with God.* There is *never* an acceptable excuse for adultery. The words of 1 John 1:8-10 were written with situations like yours in mind: "If we claim to be without sin, we deceive ourselves and the truth is not in us. If we confess our sins, he is faithful and just and will forgive us our sins and purify us from all unrighteousness. If we claim we have not sinned, we make him out to be a liar and his word has no place in our lives."

The good news is that God's grace is available to you, too. But you must admit your sin to God, agree that what you're doing is wrong, and turn away from it. These things may be difficult, but if you are submitting to the Holy Spirit in order to do the right thing, you can draw upon His power.

Next, realize that if your mate doesn't know about your adultery, there is no biblical requirement (thus, no universal leading of the Spirit) that you confess it to him or her. Ask yourself honestly what your reason would be for such a confession. If it's only to "get it out" and relieve the pressure of deception on yourself, you might feel better afterward, but you might also destroy your spouse in the process.

Tell your mate only when you're convinced the Holy Spirit wants you to do so—when you can honestly say it's the best thing for your spouse (for health reasons, for example) and your marriage, in spite of the pain the revelation will cause.

If your mate does know about your infidelity, the Spirit wants you to seek his or her forgiveness. Go in humility and repentance. Be patient and sensitive to your partner's emotional pain. It may take him or her some time, and also, perhaps, some good Christian counseling to work through the issues and the feelings before reaching a place of being able to forgive you. Give your mate time while you stay humble and prayerful before God.

Rebuilding Security

It almost goes without saying that you must also commit yourself to faithfulness from this point forward. You must assure your spouse that it won't happen again. And then, to help you keep that promise, you must walk with the Spirit moment by moment, day by day.

You must also be prepared to take steps, perhaps drastic steps, to avoid further temptation. You might need to stop traveling in your job if being on the road could contribute to another moral failure. You might need to change jobs altogether, especially if the person with whom you had the affair was a coworker. You might also need to make yourself regularly accountable to a pastor, counselor, or trustworthy (but tough) friend who will ask you the hard, direct questions about how you're doing in this area. However difficult it may be to do any of these things, we assure you the price will be well worth it if, in the process, you can save your marriage.

The Spirit is always—even in the best of times— leading you to pray for your spouse, but that's especially important now. Pray for these things for him or her: healing from the emotional and spiritual pain, an openness to the Spirit and His leading, a growing tenderness toward you, and a reconciliation in the marriage.

Finally, if your mate forgives you and receives you back, be slow and sensitive in rebuilding the relationship. Life will almost certainly be strained for a while. Be patient. Assure your spouse often of your love and devotion. Be especially careful in resuming physical intimacy. It needs to happen, but it will probably be difficult and awkward at first, so be understanding, patient, and gentle. Bathe all aspects of your relationship, but particularly this one, in prayer.

Adultery is one of the worst things that can happen to a marriage. But with the Spirit's help, as both partners submit to His leading and empowering, it can be survived, and the relationship can be rebuilt and perhaps, in time, become even stronger than before. If there has been unfaithfulness in your marriage, we pray that this will be your experience.

Heavenly Father,

I know from Your Word there is no sin I have ever committed that You cannot forgive. Even when I have been unfaithful to You, You have continued to love—and You have forgiven me.

May the Holy Spirit empower me to forgive even the most difficult offenses. By Your grace may I not consider any sin against me unforgivable.

In the Savior's name. Amen.

16

When We Don't See Eye to Eye

Just a few days ago, a friend of ours, Sean, had an experience that could have easily developed into a major conflict between him and his wife. It started out as a simple, ordinary household accident—no big deal. But when emotions get involved and we're not listening to the Holy Spirit, such situations can escalate rapidly into hurtful disputes.

Here's what happened. Sean had set a large water pitcher on the kitchen counter, near the sink. His wife, Erin, knowing that company was coming soon, was busy cleaning and straightening the house, including the kitchen. At one point, as she went to rinse out her cleaning rag in the sink, she bumped that pitcher and knocked it onto the floor, where it broke and spilled water everywhere—under the stove, under the refrigerator, under the counters—you get the idea.

Of course, since Erin was hurriedly getting the house ready for guests, this was the last thing she needed. So even though Sean immediately came to her rescue and tried to help sop up the water, she was a little, shall we say, upset with the situation. And in her frustration, as she was on her hands and knees, mopping up water, she said to him, "If you had put that pitcher away in the refrigerator like you were supposed to, this wouldn't have happened!"

Critical moment alert!

How was Sean going to respond to that accusation? What he said or did next would either defuse the situation, leading to peace, or escalate it, leading to a full-blown conflict.

"My first reaction," Sean told us in describing the incident, "was to get defensive. I thought, *Wait a minute! The pitcher was right there in plain view. It's not as if it snuck up on you! You're the one who knocked it over! Don't try to pin the blame on me!*"

His thoughts and feelings were understandable, even predictable, weren't they? And if we had been in his place, most of us, most of the time, would have been strongly tempted to put those thoughts into words. After all, the world says, "Stand up for your rights! Don't let anyone falsely accuse you!" The flesh says, "Don't let her pin this on you. If you do, you might never hear the end of it. Besides, it's not fair!" And the devil says, "Are you going to let her get away with that? What kind of man are you, anyway? Imagine what the guys in the locker room would say!"

But if Sean did put his thoughts into words, adding fuel to the fire, Erin might come back with something like,

"You knew it should be put away! How many times do I have to tell you? Do you think I'm your slave or something?" And the situation would have gone rapidly downhill, each of them getting more defensive with each successive round of accusations.

It's the Little Things

It's amazing how quickly the simplest minor irritations can become major conflicts between two people who love each other and live together as husband and wife. One person likes things neat and tidy; the other prefers a little "friendly" clutter. One person never forgets to put the cap back on the toothpaste tube; the other never remembers. One person is content to go to McDonald's whenever they eat out; the other is sick and tired of burgers and fries, not to mention the sight of golden arches.

Any of these differences, which create minor irritations, can easily produce a blow-up if they're not dealt with under the leading of the Holy Spirit. All it takes is one word, one hurtful gesture, one insensitive response to spark a conflict into flame.

When conflict is allowed to flourish,
we seldom get to the real matters that divide us.
In addition, conflicts raging out of control
tend to produce emotional scars
that take a long time to heal.

As we've looked back over our own 20-plus years of marriage, we've realized that most of our fights have not been over major issues. Typically they've been over petty issues that, in the end, didn't even get resolved because our disagreement became the bigger issue.

When conflict is allowed to flourish, we seldom get to the real matters that divide us. In addition, conflicts raging out of control tend to produce emotional scars that take a long time to heal. We think we forget hurtful words said in the heat of the moment (or at least that our spouse will), but those words have a way of sticking in the heart and mind, causing pain for a long time to come.

In the same way, our hostile exchanges can create a great deal of insecurity. In one verbal confrontation I had with Teri, I angrily mentioned the word *divorce*. This struck a deep fear in Teri's heart because she didn't know how serious I was at that moment, or what our future relationship would be like, even if I wasn't serious about separating.

That exchange hurt Teri so deeply, in fact, that in its aftermath, when we had both calmed down, we agreed never to mention divorce again, no matter how heated the exchange. And we never have. (Death, yes! Divorce, no!)

                                    ⋙

Marriages marked by repeated, unrestrained, and especially unresolved conflict will be very insecure. That, in turn, undermines intimacy. After all, if you live in fear and are constantly hurt by the person closest to you, you want to pull away for safety's sake. You certainly don't want to draw near.

Even in the short term, when conflict is only occasional, discord is still the enemy of intimacy, including the physical relationship. In our marriage, for example, John tends to bounce back from a battle quickly, thinking everything is okay. But I need more time to regroup emotionally. I do not mean days, or even hours—remember, we make the decision to forgive each other rather than grow bitter. But John is very sensitive to my emotions, realizing I might benefit from a little space before an affectionate embrace.

∽

This aftermath period presents another critical moment in the marriage. When the conflict is over and one partner is ready to enjoy the sexual relationship but the other isn't, how will each of them respond? Depending on the answers, the marriage can be greatly strengthened or greatly damaged at that point.

A Way with Words

Please understand that conflict in a marriage is a very serious issue. Arguments are inevitable between any two people, especially when they share as much time and space as husbands and wives do. But when friction is handled in such a way that it creates pain in one or both spouses, or when disagreements aren't dealt with and the hurt accumulates and grows, the world, the flesh, and Satan really go to work, tearing down the foundation of the relationship.

The signs of this are clear: Where once there was love and affection, there's now hostility. Where once harmony prevailed, now disputes are commonplace. Where once peace was the norm, now angry outbursts are standard, even to the point of becoming verbal and emotional abuse.

It's our sad observation, from talking with hundreds of couples, that verbal abuse is nearing epidemic proportions in Christian marriages. In some cases, it even leads to physical abuse.

Any abuse grieves the Holy Spirit deeply, more than words can convey. What could be further from the instruction to husbands in His Word, "Husbands, love your wives, just as Christ loved the church and gave himself up for her. . . . Each one of you also must love his wife as he loves himself" (Ephesians 5:25, 33). Likewise, how can abusive talk or behavior be consistent with the admonition to wives, "The wife must respect her husband" (Ephesians 5:33). And husbands and wives, as well as all other Christians, are commanded by God, "Do not let any unwholesome talk come out of your mouths, but *only what is helpful for building others up* according to their needs, that it may benefit those who listen" (Ephesians 4:29, emphasis added).

∽∞∽

I wonder how many marriages would be saved if we would follow this simple but wise admonition before speaking to our spouses, particularly in the heat of the moment. As we've stated earlier, most of our disagreements originate with trivial matters, and then build with one cutting remark followed by another. I have seen this cycle abruptly broken in our rela-

tionship as John has said something to purposely build me up rather than cut me down. It is both humbling and healing.

❦

That's the direct opposite of abusive speech, isn't it? It's also a tough standard. In fact, it's one we can live up to only with the leading and power of the Holy Spirit.

In the next chapter, we'll look closely at how the Spirit can help us resolve our conflicts and restore peace, harmony, and love to our homes.

Dear heavenly Father,

I confess that there are times when I have allowed my self-centered agenda to become a point of contention in my marriage. Please forgive me and show me how I can remain under the Spirit's control when _____ (spouse) and I disagree.

Help me to avoid conflict with _____ (spouse) that is unnecessary and tends to escalate.

Give me a sensitivity to and respect for _____ (spouse's) opinions and insights.

I ask these things in Jesus' name. Amen.

17

Keeping Conflict Under Control

At one level, the way to keep conflict under control sounds deceptively simple. But of course it's not; if it were, there would be a lot less pain and tension in most Christian marriages. To get a snapshot view of how controlling conflict works, let's return to the story of Sean and Erin from the preceding chapter. Then we'll examine more closely the dynamics of what happened.

You'll recall that Sean and Erin had experienced an accident in their kitchen. Erin, upset, frustrated, and expecting company to arrive at any minute, vented at Sean, accusing him of being responsible for the mess on her kitchen floor. And Sean, feeling he was being unfairly accused, had an initial *internal* response of wanting to defend himself and tell her just what he thought of her accusation. We'll pick up the story from there.

"As soon as she blamed me for the accident," Sean said, "I wanted to say, 'What! The pitcher was right there in plain sight! How is it *my* fault that you bumped it and knocked it off the counter?' "

But before he said anything, he sensed the Holy Spirit leading him in a different direction.

Gentleness is not weakness; it's not rolling over;
it is not trying to imitate a doormat.
Gentleness is strength clothed in tranquility.

"I realized she was just upset," Sean said. "She would probably let it go soon if I didn't add fuel to the fire. On the other hand, I knew that defending myself, trying to put the blame back on her, wouldn't help anything. In fact, almost anything I tried to say—even trying to explain things as logically or objectively as I could—wouldn't work. Under the circumstances, it would only escalate her feelings and create an even worse situation."

Even though his pride and ego and sense of fairness screamed at him to strike back at Erin, Sean responded calmly. "I said a quick 'Lord, help me' prayer, bit my tongue, and didn't respond to her accusation at all," Sean said. "I helped her a little more with the clean-up, then got out of the way to let her work off her frustration."

And the result?

"A few minutes later, the water was all sopped up, we were both calmed down, and Erin was even joking about the whole incident," Sean added.

The conflict was resolved almost as soon as it began.

In a word, the key to Sean's successful, marriage-building response was *gentleness*. Under the leading and empowering of the Holy Spirit, he treated Erin gently in a conflict situation. If a marriage is to survive long-term, and especially if it's going to *thrive*, at least one spouse— but ideally both—must make a habit of responding this way. "The fruit of the Spirit is [self-sacrificing] love ... peace, patience ... *gentleness* and self-control" (Galatians 5:22,23, emphasis added). The alternative, which is habitually responding with harsh words or actions, is outside the will of God, dishonoring to each other, and a cancer on the relationship that will more than likely kill it, later if not sooner.

Countering Conflict

Gentleness is strength clothed in tranquility. Contrary to the common misconception, gentleness is not weakness; it's not rolling over; it's not being a Casper Milquetoast; it's not trying to imitate a doormat. In the New Testament particularly, *gentleness* usually refers to a controlled and deliberate response, especially in the face of a personal offense by which one could easily be provoked. It means being calm and gracious when the natural tendency is to lash out and return insult for insult, injury for injury. It *does not* mean accepting mistreatment from your spouse with resignation; it *does* mean a supernatural capacity to refrain from responding harshly and escalating the level of conflict.

When we look at gentleness this way, we can see how Sean's response provides a good example. He chose not to respond in anger to Erin's statement. He also didn't grovel and lay any blame. Instead, he defused the situation by relying on the Holy Spirit to control his emotions, keep him quiet, and give Erin time to let her feelings cool down.

The Bible gives us other good illustrations as well. Moses was one of the most prominent and powerful people ever to walk the face of this earth. Trained in Egypt to be a member of the pharaoh's ruling family, he became an outcast when he killed an Egyptian who was battering one of his fellow Israelites. Later, God used him to do miracle after miracle in Egypt, culminating in Israel's deliverance from bondage. Directed by God, Moses parted the Red Sea, received the Ten Commandments from the finger of God, led the Israelite people for 40 years, and enjoyed a face-to-face relationship with the Lord.

Yet Moses was also a gentle (humble) man: "Now Moses was a very humble man, more humble than anyone else on the face of the earth" (Numbers 12:3). We can see it in the way he related to the people of Israel. When they questioned Moses' leadership, trying his patience and love for them time after time, God threatened to destroy them, but Moses always interceded for them, asking God to forgive them. He never attacked them, never sought to get even.

Jesus also demonstrated gentleness. Consider the day when He rode triumphantly into Jerusalem. The prophet Zechariah had foretold that day centuries before: "Rejoice greatly, O Daughter of Zion! Shout, Daughter of Jerusalem!

See, your king comes to you, righteous and having salvation, gentle and riding on a donkey, on a colt, the foal of a donkey" (Zechariah 9:9). And that's just how it happened. He entered the city on the back of a donkey.

Note the contrasting elements. Jesus was their King, the God of the universe, the all-powerful and all-knowing One. But He didn't charge into the city on a massive, magnificent war horse, leading an army of mighty men. No, He came gently, calmly, slowly, riding on a donkey.

Jesus Himself spoke of His nature when He issued this well-known invitation: "Come to me, all you who are weary and burdened, and I will give you rest. Take my yoke upon you and learn from me, for I am *gentle* and humble in heart, and you will find rest for your souls" (Matthew 11:28,29, emphasis added). Gentleness, then, is part of the very character of God, a part of the fruit of the Spirit working in our lives, and an aspect of what Jesus meant when He said, "When the Counselor comes, whom I will send to you from the Father, the Spirit of truth who goes out from the Father, he will testify about me" (John 15:26).

A Spirit-Directed Response

If just one partner in a marriage can maintain a spirit of gentleness as conflict develops, the disagreement can usually be worked out in a way that builds the relationship. Here are some specific guidelines for making that happen:

- First and foremost, listen and respond to the inner voice of the Holy Spirit. Let Him lead you down the path of gentleness rather than going on your own path of getting even.

- Second, asking for the Spirit's help, keep looking at the situation through His eyes and heart—His eyes of love for your spouse and His heart's desire to strengthen and heal the relationship. Don't give ground to the enemy, allowing your thoughts to turn to how unfair things are or how you could put your mate in his or her place.

- Third, under the power of the Spirit don't allow yourself to blow your cork, and *do not*, regardless of how heated the discussion, use profanity. Instead, turn your thinking 180 degrees and ask, "How can I encourage my spouse in this situation? How can I show love?"

Imagine what would happen in most conflicts if both partners started thinking this way!

∽∞∾

In our marriage, growing in this direction of handling disputes with gentleness has been a long and tough process. We're not suggesting it's something you develop overnight, either individually or as a couple. For most of us (there are always exceptions), there's no supernatural switch, where all you have to do is find it, flip it, and all will be well. Personally, John and I still don't do gentleness perfectly ourselves. Even today there are times when we take matters into our own hands, blow up, and say things we shouldn't, hurting each other. By God's grace and the growth we've experienced in listening and submitting to the Holy Spirit, however, these times are now far less frequent than they used to be. Our relationship is much more healthy and enjoyable as a result.

By that same grace which is extended to you and your marriage, this same experience can also be yours.

Heavenly Father,

I know that when _____ (spouse) and I have a disagreement and we lash out at each other, You are there; and You are disappointed when we don't turn to You for help. Please forgive me for ignoring You or for refusing Your direct intervention.

Knowing that times of conflict are an opportunity for the flesh or even for demonic forces, I want to surrender control to Your Spirit during these tense moments. Please guard my heart, my mind, and my lips so that I do not sin against You or against my mate.

These things I ask in Jesus' precious name. Amen.

18

Who, Me?
Submit?

Tom and Sonya have a problem. As a dating and then engaged couple, all seemed to go smoothly. Sonya was deeply in love, and she happily followed Tom's lead in everything. They went where he wanted to go, saw the movies he wanted to see, and did the things he wanted to do—mostly sports of one kind or another. When they talked, if she disagreed with any of Tom's opinions, she never said so.

Sonya and Tom never discussed this pattern, because neither of them gave it much thought. They just assumed that everything was fine and that if any major disagreements ever arose, love would conquer all. Now they're married, and neither one of them is very happy.

Because of their widely differing personalities and backgrounds, they disagree often and loudly. And with the glow long gone from their relationship, Sonya has ceased pretending to support Tom's every opinion or decision.

Tom has grown fond of quoting Ephesians 5:22-24 to his wife: "Wives, submit to your husbands as to the Lord. For the husband is the head of the wife as Christ is the head of the church, his body, of which he is the Savior. Now as the church submits to Christ, so also wives should submit to their husbands in everything." He first heard it in a sermon shortly after their marriage, and now he can't seem to recite it too often.

Actually, he only quotes the first sentence from the passage, but it's enough, given the way he uses it—like a hammer to beat his wife into obedience—to make her roll her eyes in disgust and even, occasionally, to question God's goodness. She also wonders if the Bible is still culturally relevant. Tom, on the other hand, thinks this "Bible stuff" is pretty neat. It gets him what he wants and restores "harmony" to their home.

In fact, however, they've *both* misunderstood a key scriptural teaching about the husband-wife relationship. As a result, they don't really resolve conflicts. Instead, Sonya puts up a fight for a while before finally, with resignation, throwing in the towel every time.

Does this description of how Tom and Sonya relate sound at all like your marriage? Their situation is extremely common in Christian homes today, and their misreading of the Bible is reinforced by many well-intentioned but misguided pastors. For husbands and wives to get along and work out their differences as the Holy Spirit desires, however, Tom's favorite passage has to be viewed in the context of the rest of Ephesians 5 and of Scripture as a whole. Ephesians 5 is *not* a license for the husband to dominate his wife. What Ephesians 5 actually teaches is *mutual* submission of the husband and wife to each other. Let us explain what we mean.

Submit to One Another

At the beginning of Ephesians 5, the apostle Paul wrote, "Be imitators of God, therefore [that's what the Spirit wants to help us do] . . . and [it means that we should] live a life of love, just as Christ loved us and gave himself up for us as a fragrant offering and sacrifice to God" (verses 1,2). All Christians, including husbands and wives, are being told to love others self-sacrificially, just like Jesus.

Then, just four verses before Tom's favorite passage, we read, "Be filled with the Spirit" (verse 18). Again, all Christians are being addressed, and we've already seen what the Holy Spirit wants to produce in us: love, joy, patience, gentleness, humility, and so on.

Does a husband who uses God's Word to "beat" his wife into obedience display these qualities? (That's a rhetorical question.)

Next, we come to verse 21, right before the part Tom likes: "Submit to one another out of reverence for Christ." Here we see the principle of mutual submission. Submission isn't a one-way street. Instead, it's supposed to work as Paul described in another of his letters: "Do nothing out of selfish ambition or vain conceit, but in humility consider others better than yourselves. Each of you should look not only to your own interests, but also to the interests of others" (Philippians 2:3,4).

Is a husband who lords it over his wife considering her better than himself and looking out for her best interests? (That's another rhetorical question.)

Then, finally, come the words that Tom likes so much. But Ephesians 5 doesn't end there. In fact, the very next verses say, "Husbands, love your wives, [How?] just as Christ loved the church and *gave himself up for her*. [There's that self-sacrifice issue again.] . . . In this same way, husbands ought to love their wives as their own bodies. He who loves his wife loves himself. After all, no one ever hated his own body, but he feeds and cares for it, just as Christ does the church" (verses 25,28,29, emphasis added).

Is a husband who always ignores his wife's desires, opinions, and insights giving himself up for her? Is he loving her the way he loves his own body? Is he following the example of Jesus Christ? (Yes, these, too, are rhetorical questions.)

These other verses from Ephesians 5 that we've just looked at put Tom's favorite passage in its fuller and proper context. If Tom has looked at them, he's choosing to ignore them. And he's ignoring the leading of the Holy Spirit in his life. But, interestingly, Sonya appears to be choosing to ignore the lesson of Tom's verses as well. They both need to understand *mutual* submission.

The Great Debate

First and foremost, as we've seen, all Christians are to be submitted to Jesus Christ through the leading of His indwelling Holy Spirit. If husbands and wives did this, most of the other issues and the debate about marital submission would never come up.

How can a husband and wife settle disagreements in an attitude of mutual submission? It begins with humility.

Second, a wife is not meant to be a slave, and a husband is not meant to be an autocratic, domineering master. When God created the first woman and brought her to her husband, it was because "it is not good for the man to be alone. I will make a helper suitable for him" (Genesis 2:18). She was to be his companion, his partner, his coworker, his completer. And they're both to be submissive to the needs of the other. Following Jesus' example, the husband should be ready to give his life for his wife—not only in some big, dramatic gesture like pushing her out of the way of an oncoming train, but also in the give-and-take of everyday marriage.

How can a husband and wife settle disagreements in an attitude of mutual submission? It begins with humility. Deep down, one partner in a marriage often thinks he or she is somehow better or smarter than the other. As long as that feeling of superiority persists, the one holding it will always be tempted to push his or her agenda on the other, believing that he or she "knows what's best for us."

The apostle Paul, however, under the inspiration of the Holy Spirit, commanded, "For by the grace given me

I say to every one of you: Do not think of yourself more highly than you ought, but rather think of yourself with sober judgment" (Romans 12:3). And in Ephesians 4:2, he said, "Be completely humble and gentle; be patient, bearing with one another in love."

Only when we obey these instructions, in the power of the Spirit, can we get our focus off ourselves and our desires, and onto the needs and desires of our partners. Then, if there's a disagreement of some kind, we can search the Scriptures together to see if they speak to the situation. We can take the time to gather further relevant information, which may lead to a harmonious resolution of the dispute. We can also pray through the possibilities together, asking God to help us reach a point of seeing eye to eye, whether the issue is parenting strategy, finances, vacation plans, or whatever.

If we still disagree after all that, however, and we can afford to wait before making a decision—even if it's only overnight—we should do so. Teri and I often find that allowing a little time to cool off and think about the issues and options helps us come to a better, more peaceable agreement.

Finally, if conflict remains and a decision needs to be made, we find ourselves back at Tom's favorite verses. In saying that the husband is the head of the wife as Christ is the head of the church, God (speaking through the apostle Paul) gave the ultimate *authority* for family decisions, as well as the *responsibility*, to the husband. In the end, someone has to make the decision, and that power rests with the husband, despite many wives' serious misgivings.

Husbands, please note that this authority should be exercised prayerfully, carefully, humbly, and with full respect for the wife's opinions and feelings. And in accepting this authority, you must also accept the responsibility. No trying to blame what proves to be a bad decision on your wife!

Yielding to her husband's authority can be difficult for the wife, especially if she's still convinced she's right. She may not like his choices; she might actually be a better decision-maker. She may continue to pray that God will change her husband's mind and heart. But when all is said and done, if the two still don't see eye to eye, the Holy Spirit is leading her to submit to Him by submitting to her husband. And if she's willing, He will empower her, no matter how difficult it may seem. And her humble submission will give the Holy Spirit time to complete a work in her husband's life as well. I have seen, more than once, a wife who is ultimately committed to God's will lovingly support her husband even though the direction he has chosen was against her better judgment. Her submission and subsequent support (rather than "I told you so"), even in the face of failure, has allowed the Holy Spirit freedom to do a changing work in the life of her husband, which has ultimately drawn them closer to Him and each other.

Taking all of Ephesians 5 into account, learning and accepting mutual submission and allowing the Spirit to produce His fruit of Christlikeness in us will bring about a peaceful resolution to most marital conflicts. This will enable us to deal with the anger in our lives, which, if left unchecked, can destroy a marriage faster than almost anything else.

Father in heaven,

I confess that I have not always submitted to You and Your will for my life. I choose now to adopt a submissive spirit.

Remove pride and arrogance from my life so I can be a humble servant to _____ (spouse).

Please teach me to love _____ (spouse) with the kind of sacrificial love the Savior demonstrated when He humbled Himself to the death on the cross.

In Jesus' name I pray. Amen.

19

Words That Burn, Words That Build

Words have incredible power. They can either build up or tear down, quench a thirsty soul or burn it like acid. This is never more true than in our relationships with those closest to us. All too often, Christian husbands and wives use words to scorch and destroy one another.

As we've noted, and as shocking as it may seem, verbal abuse appears to be at a near-epidemic level—even in Christian marriages. It's easy for believing couples to dress up, put on a pretty face, drive to church, hear a message from the Bible, and then return home to hack each other to pieces with their words.

I have frequently looked out at a congregation from the platform on a Sunday morning, seeing many dignified men and charming women, and wondered what might be taking place behind the closed doors of their houses. All too often, the scene would be in stark contrast to the smooth, well-scrubbed look presented in the pews of our churches.

We don't believe that Christians really want to live that way. Sadly, many aren't even aware of the patterns into which they've fallen. Or if they are, they can't seem to break the habit. How can we get free from the chains of harsh words and begin to control our words so their impact on our marriages is positive rather than destructive?

Quick to Listen, Slow to Speak

The Holy Spirit has given us this counsel: "My dear brothers, take note of this: Everyone should be quick to listen, slow to speak" (James 1:19). The basic principle is that we need to learn restraint, to reflect on what's best or most appropriate *before* we say anything rather than just reacting "off the top of our heads." For instance, a wife models a new dress for her husband and asks, "What do you think?" The typical husband will instantly respond, without thinking, "It's all right. How much did it cost?"

That might be called insensitivity more than verbal abuse, but it sends a message, nonetheless, that he's more interested in money than he is in her feelings. A steady diet of such verbal signals will have a gradual, corrosive effect on her confidence and on their relationship.

A greater, more immediate effect will be felt in a situation like this: Early in the morning, as a wife is just getting out of bed and walking toward the bathroom, she trips over her husband's shirt worn the day before. Last night, as he did his Michael Jordan jump-shot imitation, the shirt landed on the floor *near* the dirty-clothes hamper, but not quite in it. For him, that was close enough.

"Why couldn't you put this shirt *in* the hamper?" she yells. "You *never* pick up after yourself! Do you think I'm your mother?!"

And he, just barely awake himself, replies sarcastically, "No, I think my mother still loves me." Then he adds more fuel to the fire: "Anyway, what's the big deal? The way you keep house, I'm surprised you even noticed one shirt on the floor."

These kinds of words go straight from our flesh to our mate's heart. That's why the Spirit continually wants to remind us to be quick to listen to Him, to the needs of our spouse, to what's ultimately in our own best interests, and be slow to speak, even (perhaps especially) when we feel provoked.

What Our Words Reveal

The Holy Spirit prods us to remember that our words reveal our character. If we claim to be followers of Jesus Christ, then we need to examine our speech to be sure it reflects His character and not our flesh. Here's what the Spirit said through the apostle James:

> With the tongue we praise our Lord and Father, and with it we curse men, who have been made in God's likeness. Out of the same mouth come praise and cursing. My brothers, this should not be. Can both fresh water and salt water flow from the same spring? My brothers, can a fig tree bear olives, or a grapevine bear figs? Neither can a salt spring produce fresh water (James 3:9-12).

There's a word for those of us who sit in church and praise God on Sunday morning, then verbally tear down our spouse on Sunday afternoon: *hypocrite*. Such vastly different kinds of speech ought not to come out of the same mouth, the Holy Spirit is telling us. We cannot go on assuming God doesn't really care about the way we talk to each other. He says to us, "Do not merely listen to the word, and so deceive yourselves. *Do what it says*" (James 1:22, emphasis added).

Small but Powerful

The Holy Spirit wants us never to forget how incredibly significant our words are. They may seem small and unimportant, especially at the moment when we say them, but most assuredly they are not. Consider these further insights:

> We all stumble in many ways. If anyone is never at fault in what he says, he is a perfect man, able to keep his whole body in check. When we put bits into the mouths of horses to make them obey us, we can turn the whole animal. Or take ships as an example. Although they are so large and are driven by strong winds, they are steered by a very small rudder wherever the pilot wants to go. Likewise the tongue is a small part of the body, but it makes great boasts (James 3:2-5).

Notice that the content of our conversation is a measure of our whole ability to live in obedience to God. James compared the tongue to a bit in the mouth of a horse; its relative size may be small, yet it can turn that mighty animal in any direction or make it stop on command. He compared the tongue to a sailing ship's rudder as well. Again, the size is small compared to the overall bulk of the great vessel, and the ship is driven by the awesome forces of nature, yet that rudder determines the course of the boat and everyone aboard.

Mean-spirited, stinging words make a staggering, lasting impact. In case you have any doubts about that, we invite you to think back to a time a year or more ago when someone really chewed you out. It might have been at home, at school, or perhaps on the job. It may have been a long conversation or just one cutting remark. But we'll bet you can remember at least one such occasion—and probably the exact words the person used to put you down. We'll bet you didn't have to think long to come up with it, either. And we're sure that the memory of that event still hurts to this day, no matter how long ago it occurred.

"I hate you!"

"I don't think I ever really loved you!"

"You're stupid!"

"You're lazy!"

"You're a lousy provider!"

"You're a lousy housekeeper!"

"You're a joke in bed!"

"Why can't you be more like . . . ?"

"I want a divorce!"

These words, and others like them, do incredible damage. Even if we regret them as soon as they slip out of our mouths, it's too late. Even if we didn't really mean them, it's too late. A wound has been created that may take years to heal. Don't ever forget the power of your words to do harm. "Reckless words pierce like a sword . . .

" . . . But the tongue of the wise brings healing" (Proverbs 12:18). This is the other side of the coin, as it were, the side we want to show to those around us. Just as the wrong words can cause great pain, so the right words can provide great comfort and restoration. "Pleasant words are a honeycomb, sweet to the soul and healing to the bones" (Proverbs 16:24). "A man finds joy in giving an apt reply—and how good is a timely word!" (Proverbs 15:23).

Can you think of a time when someone said something to you that was "just right"—just what you needed to hear at that moment? Perhaps a word of praise, a piece of great advice, or an expression of affection when you were feeling unloved? We hope you can, although it's human nature to remember negative events more easily and sharply. And if you can, hasn't that also had a lasting impact for good? "A word aptly spoken is like apples of gold in settings of silver" (Proverbs 25:11). Never forget the power of your words to do good.

Please realize that the way you speak is a matter of supernatural consequence. Words are primary weapons in the spiritual warfare that's raging right here and now. If your tongue is controlled by God, it will express the fruit of the Spirit. But the opposite is also true: "Consider what a great forest is set on fire by a small spark. The tongue also is a fire, a world of evil among the parts of the body. It corrupts the whole person, sets the whole course of his life on fire, and *is itself set on fire by hell*" (James 3:5,6, emphasis added).

The next time you hear someone—including yourself—say something cruel, selfish, demeaning, or otherwise hurtful, you won't have to guess where the inspiration for it came from! We ask you, who do you want to be in control of your tongue, the Lord or the devil? It's your choice.

The Tongue Tamer

As with the other aspects of living for God in your marriage, rely on the power of the indwelling Spirit to control your tongue. "All kinds of animals, birds, reptiles and creatures of the sea are being tamed and have been tamed by man, but no man can tame the tongue. It is a restless evil, full of deadly poison" (James 3:7,8).

Again, we simply can't do it on our own. We can tame dogs, cats, snakes, tigers, and even killer whales, but we can't tame our tongue in our own strength. We're too quick to say the first thing that comes to mind; too quick to get defensive and strike back when provoked; too quick to seek what we perceive to be our own best interests; and too slow to recognize that we're involved in an ongoing spiritual struggle.

How can the Spirit lead and strengthen us in this area? First, if we have failed consistently with our words in the past, even to the point of abuse, He would have us go to our spouse (and children, if necessary) and make things right. That means asking for forgiveness, vowing not to do it anymore, making ourselves accountable to them for our future conduct, and giving them permission to lovingly but pointedly take us to task if they hear us slipping into our old, abusive habits.

Second, many years ago, the Spirit led us to adopt a practice that we recommend to you as well. As soon as we awaken each morning, before we say anything to each other or anyone else, we turn our first words toward heaven. In prayer, we ask the Lord to control what we say that day. We commit our words to Him, praying that we will only build up and not tear down those with whom we come in contact. We've found that beginning the day this way has been a big help in keeping us sensitive to the potential impact of our words and the need to be quick to listen and slow to speak.

Third, the Spirit wants us to be aware of those critical moments in the day when our hackles rise or our tempers flare and the hurtful words start to fly. Unless we're alert to those moments, the words can come before we know it. But in those times, He is telling us to stay under His control, to offer a gentle answer that turns away wrath, to say only words that build up rather than words that tear down. And we need to learn to listen for His soothing voice amid the turbulence of our emotions.

Are Teri and I perfect in our speech? Hardly. But by God's grace and with His help—and only because of His help—we're much healthier in this area than we used to be. So take heart: If there was hope for us in controlling our tongues, there's hope for you and your marriage as well.

Heavenly Father,
I ask that Your Holy Spirit would give me a deeper understanding of the impact of my words toward my mate. Reveal to me how my words have hurt _____

(spouse) and have threatened to light a fire of bitterness within.

Please bring my words under Your Spirit's control so that they become a source of blessing to _____ (spouse).

I ask this in the Savior's name. Amen.

20

Making Sense of the Sensual

Sarah, a dear Christian woman, loved her husband very much. In spite of that love, however, she recoiled at the thought of physical intimacy with him. That made Harold feel rejected and caused Sarah, in turn, to feel guilty. When she came to us for help, her marriage was in serious trouble.

The Song of Solomon in the Old Testament was written by the wisest man who ever lived. It is a celebration of sexual love within the bonds of matrimony. The book moves from the engagement phase of the relationship to the wedding night, and then on to a mature love. Throughout, it extols the loving desire of a husband for his wife and of a wife for her husband.

Unfortunately, from the calls and letters we receive at our ministry, as well as our counseling experiences, we can only conclude that few Christian couples are singing the Song of Songs. Instead, many are singing a song of sexual sorrows.

In this chapter and the next, we want to deal with two common problem situations. First we'll deal with sexual dysfunction, where both partners in the marriage desire physical intimacy, but for some reason it just isn't working. Then we'll deal with those cases where intimacy is possible, but the husband and wife have different levels of desire. We are convinced that even in this most intimate aspect of your relationship the Holy Spirit wants to provide guidance and encouragement.

Obstacles to Intimacy

When the longing for intimacy is present in both husband and wife but something blocks its fulfillment, it's vital that they discover what that something is. Only by learning the cause can they find a way around it. In some cases, the problem will be an obvious physical condition that makes sex difficult, painful, or even impossible. Such a condition can be hard to deal with even if it's only temporary. If it's chronic, the problem becomes even more of an emotional, physical, and spiritual challenge for the couple.

A second reason some couples don't enjoy sex is that there has been some past trauma that remains unresolved. When a person has been victimized sexually, emotional and spiritual issues (such as, "Why did God let this happen?") must be faced. If they're not dealt with under the Spirit's guidance, a person can remain in bondage for years. This is what had happened to Sarah. As a child, she had been abused repeatedly by her stepfather. She had buried the feelings of shame and bitterness and pain for years, never facing them until they threatened to undo her marriage. This was a spiritual stronghold in her life that Satan wanted to maintain to keep her from freedom in Christ.

Another obstacle to enjoyment of marital sex is past sexual sin. Consider the case of Jeff and Martha. Before they married, Jeff had remained a virgin, but Martha had been promiscuous. A couple of months into their marriage, they were having major problems with intimacy. Why? Martha tried to blame it on Jeff's inexperience, creating a false guilt in him. But the fact was that she struggled with her own unresolved guilt over her premarital conduct.

When Martha turned down Jeff's sexual overtures for about the tenth time, things went from bad to worse. Jeff was now feeling rejected and hurt, and for the first time he began to lash out verbally at Martha. "What's the matter?" he taunted. "Don't I measure up to the guys you had before me?"

His remark, obviously meant to hurt Martha the way he was hurting, hit the bullseye. Now Martha felt even more guilty—and incapable of enjoying sex.

Sometimes the problem is that the couple had sex with each other before they were married. They try to rationalize their behavior by saying, "Well, we figured we were going to get married, and we did. We just got started a little early." But in their heart of hearts, one or both of them knows that what they did was wrong. Since glossing over sin with excuses doesn't work, that couple also struggles with guilt.

One more obstacle to sexual fulfillment that we've seen fairly often is that some Christians don't understand how positive God is about sex in marriage. In fact, they think it's something dirty and ugly, a view that's not only unhealthy but also unbiblical.

Tami, a pastor's wife, is a good example of this attitude. As a young girl growing up on a farm, she had the normal childish curiosity about the physical differences between the sexes. But her parents responded to her questions with threats instead of answers, so she stopped asking.

One day when her parents were gone, her ten-year-old brother encouraged her to join him in taking off their clothes behind the barn, just so they could see what the other looked like. They did it and then quickly got dressed again.

When their parents got home, Tami was so scared they would discover what she had done that she finally blurted out a confession. The parents went ballistic, screaming at her and her brother about how "dirty" they were, how could they do such a thing, and so on. Then they took a belt to her brother and gave him the hardest beating of his life.

Thirty years later, now a married woman, Tami could still hear her parents' and her brother's screams as if they had happened yesterday. And she still thought of sex, even within marriage, as something dirty and ugly, something to be ashamed about. Not surprisingly, she avoided intimacy with her husband as much as possible, and when they did come together, her discomfort was obvious, which ruined the experience for both of them.

A Growing Threat

A few years ago, in an anonymous survey, some of the people attending a national Christian men's conference were asked whether they had looked at pornography in the month or two prior to the event. Keep in mind that these men were sufficiently interested in growing as Christians to put aside the time, expense, and effort to attend a conference expressly for that purpose.

Of these men, how many do you think admitted to purposely viewing pornography in the recent past? If you guessed 10 percent, you guessed too low. If you guessed 20 percent, you guessed too low. How about 30 percent? 40? In fact, the figure was more than 50 percent.

That number is shocking and disturbing. Unfortunately, it's not surprising. Many of the modern statistics about immoral behavior show little difference between Christians and non-Christians because, as we've mentioned, believers are living in the power of the flesh rather than the power of the Spirit.

Furthermore, modern American culture—the "world" —is saturated with sex. Television programs, commercials, music, movies, newspaper and magazines ads, billboards—the list goes on and on—are all filled with images of scantily clad women and sexual innuendo. Add to that the fact that men are visually stimulated. Then throw in the easy availability of so-called soft-porn magazines, movies, and videos, and you will see why it's a struggle for many men in today's culture to keep their thought lives pure. Both husbands and wives need to deal with this reality, recognizing that pornography is not harmless, but rather that it is bad for the men who use it, their wives, and their marriages. It demeans a man's wife when he thinks sexual thoughts about other women. It makes sex into an act that is entirely self-centered. There's considerable evidence that pornography is a progressive addiction. Most importantly, while feeding the desires of the sinful flesh, pornography freezes a man's desire for the Spirit.

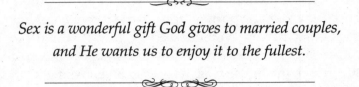

Sex is a wonderful gift God gives to married couples, and He wants us to enjoy it to the fullest.

If you are struggling with pornography, call it what it is—sin—and renounce any stronghold the enemy has as a result of your thinking and your relationship with your wife. If your natural sexual desires have been driven to the extreme and you have placed unreasonable demands on your wife, apologize and commit yourself to maintaining her dignity.

As Christian couples, we should not only renounce perversion but also prudishness. Remember, sex is a wonderful gift God gives to married couples, and He wants us to enjoy it to the fullest. We must maintain dignity while experiencing freedom of sexual expression. As long as we are honoring one another, we have great latitude in our physical expression of love for each other.

Faithful and Free

This whole area of sexuality is very sensitive because our needs are so great, and our feelings can be easily hurt. Accordingly, when we struggle in this area, the Holy Spirit wants more than anything to produce His peace, patience, kindness, gentleness, goodness, and self-control in us. We need those qualities in order to deal with the problems in a loving and healthy way while remaining faithful to each other in the marriage.

If the obstacle to sexual enjoyment is physical, there's no shame in going to a qualified doctor or counselor to see if there's a way around the problem. If intercourse simply isn't possible for some reason, perhaps another mutually enjoyable way of satisfying each other's needs can be found. We shouldn't conclude that our sex life is over without exploring all these options.

If the obstacle is a past trauma, the Spirit is asking the person who was hurt to forgive the offender. This is very hard, we know, but there is no freedom while we hang on to an offense and harbor bitterness in our hearts.

This was the situation Sarah faced. Once the Holy Spirit, through prayer, revealed to her why she was struggling so much to enjoy sex, she had to choose whether or not to forgive her stepfather for abusing her. "He doesn't deserve it!" she said, and she was right. But *she needed to forgive him* for her own sake and the sake of her marriage. Finally, as she asked the Spirit for His help, she was able to forgive her stepfather and mean it. Satan's stronghold in her life was broken, and she and her marriage began to heal.

If the problem with intimacy is that we're the guilty party because of past sexual sin, like Martha, we need to deal with that before God. The Spirit reminds us, "If we confess our sins, he is faithful and just and will forgive us our sins and purify us from all unrighteousness" (1 John 1:9). If we confess, *He forgives and purifies.* We are no longer guilty. In God's eyes, we are clean and holy and free to get on with our lives in spiritual and emotional health. "As far as the east is from the west, so far has he removed our transgressions from us" (Psalm 103:12).

Our guilt is gone! In Christ, we are made whole so that we can enjoy abundant life. That includes every part of our lives, even our physical relationship in marriage. To experience that freedom, take a few minutes, and ask the Spirit to be your Counselor and reveal to your mind any sexual sins you may have committed. Confess to Him whatever sins He brings to your mind, and then claim the forgiveness of Jesus and the cross. Then, if those sins ever come to your mind again (as they may well do), immediately take those accusatory thoughts to the Lord, and tell Him you're grateful for His forgiveness. Remember, such thoughts come from the enemy, not from God. Revelation 12:10 calls Satan "the accuser of our brothers, who accuses them before our God day and night."

Finally, if the problem is that we think intimacy is something bad, the Spirit wants to lead us back to the Word—to the Song of Solomon, which *celebrates sexual love in marriage.* He also leads us to the Genesis account of Adam and Eve *before* they fell into sin. When God brought them together, they were "naked and not ashamed," and He told them to "be fruitful and multiply." These and other passages make it clear that God created sex, and that He intended it not only for procreation, but also as a way to bring husband and wife together in the deepest level of intimacy—of knowing and being known by each other—and mutual enjoyment (see also Deuteronomy 24:5 and Proverbs 5:18,19).

When we led Tami in a study of these passages, and she saw for the first time, right there in God's Word, that sex is not dirty and ugly, it was as if a light suddenly went on in her head. As much as she loved them, she now realized her parents had been wrong about this. Marital sex is clean, beautiful, and a gift from God to be richly enjoyed. That understanding began the healing of her heart and her marriage.

So is there anything standing in the way of your full enjoyment of this wonderful gift from God? If there is, the Holy Spirit wants to reveal it and help you to remove it. Prayerfully appeal to the Holy Spirit to bring to your mind any obstacle to experiencing true physical intimacy in your marriage. If you are the one who is struggling, by faith ask Him for help and expect Him to bring about change. If the problem is your partner, ask for insight and divine sensitivity that you might be a catalyst for change in his or her life.

Once you have appealed to the Holy Spirit, speak with your partner as you sense the Spirit's leading. You will be amazed at what will happen with the Spirit's help as you begin to communicate openly and honestly with your spouse. You are on the path to true, sexual satisfaction as God intends.

Dear heavenly Father,

You have given physical intimacy as a precious gift to every married couple. Purge me of any wrong attitudes or beliefs that hinder my ability to enjoy this gift. I look to the Holy Spirit to reveal anything in the past that I need to confess or renounce in order to walk in sexual freedom.

Please make our sexual oneness all that You want it to be.

I ask this in the name of the Lord Jesus Christ. Amen.

21

Sex and the Spirit-Filled Couple

After a long and difficult day at the office, Harry returns to his castle. He walks in through the mud room, devoid of mind and emotion. His body makes its way into the living room, where it offers the usual greeting: "What's for dinner?" Then it burps its way through the meal, after which it collapses in front of the TV.

Just as the late news is ending, Harry's body, with its semicomatose brain, begins to stir. In a matter of moments, it is taken over by powerful, unrelenting desires. The late-night Olympic torch has been lit, fueled with a burst of testosterone.

Searching for the object of his craving, Harry stumbles into the arena of romance, only to find his Lady Gwenivere dozing, worn out by the activities of a hectic day and feeling no desire for anything other than sleep. Undaunted, he makes his way to the foot of the bed.

Gwenivere hears the rustling, half opens two blurry eyes, and gazes at the shadowy figure a few feet away. A burglar? No such luck.

"Are you asleep?" he whispers.

In her not-quite-awake state, she reasons, "If I say yes, I'll be lying. If I say no, he'll want what I'm not interested in giving right now. If I say nothing, maybe he'll go away." So she rolls over and buries her head in the pillow.

Then comes what seems to Harry to be an eternal silence, followed by the unmistakable sounds of deep sleep. Harry takes a ragged breath and begins to stuff his longings. He doesn't understand how Gwenivere could just fall asleep, especially since she knew what he wanted. He feels rejected, so he crawls into bed next to her, turns away from her, and broods until he finally falls asleep himself.

In the next day's early-morning rush, Harry and Gwen never say a word about what happened (or, more accurately, didn't happen) the night before. He has buried his sense of rejection, and she has stopped wondering how he could be so insensitive and unreasonable. They go into their day with little hope that the coming night will be anything more than a repeat of the one before.

Different Levels of Desire

Clearly, Harry and Gwen have different levels of sexual desire, with his appetite being the stronger. Although there are many exceptions, it's common for one partner to have a higher level of desire, and it's usually the husband. This fact tends to create a lot of frustration in both spouses.

*God expects both husband and wife to have strong sexual
desires and to find complete satisfaction in the marital bed.*

This is no small matter, because so much of our sense
of acceptance is tied up in the sexual relationship and how
we view ourselves in that area of life. The desire for sex is
so basic and so strong that God presents it as a duty that
husbands and wives owe to each other: "The husband
should fulfill his marital duty to his wife, and likewise the
wife to her husband" (1 Corinthians 7:3). While sex is
meant to be pleasurable for both partners, it's also an obligation. Some wives absolutely hate this passage, while
some husbands have made it their life's verse and quote
it to their mates constantly!

Through the apostle Paul, God goes on to reinforce the
idea: "The wife's body does not belong to her alone but
also to her husband. In the same way, the husband's body
does not belong to him alone but also to his wife" (1 Corinthians 7:4). So husband and wife have ownership rights
over the other's body; it's not just a matter of what "I"
want or what "I" feel like doing.

Please note that this is a two-way street. God expects
both husband and wife to have strong sexual desires and
to find complete satisfaction in the marital bed.

To drive home the point one more time, God says,
"Do not deprive each other except by mutual consent
and for a time, so that you may devote yourselves to
prayer. Then come together again so that Satan will not

tempt you because of your lack of self-control" (1 Corinthians 7:5). This suggests that sex should happen frequently, because even otherwise-happily-married
couples can be tempted to unfaithfulness if they go too
long without physical oneness.

Here's how we paraphrase this verse: "Don't say no
when your partner wants to have sex unless you have
agreed to a time of sexual fasting to devote yourselves to
prayer. And, as important as prayer is, don't extend this
fast for too long because Satan will use this time, when
your desire for intimacy is heightened because you haven't
been together, to tempt you sexually."

Don't those three verses in 1 Corinthians make an incredible passage? How practical can you get? In this day
of common sexual temptation and promiscuity, not
having a healthy sexual relationship in your marriage
can be very dangerous. Don't take this admonition
lightly, however uncomfortable it may make you feel.
God made us, and He knows how strong the sexual urge
is and how easily we can be tempted. Satan knows it, too.
Whether we're aware of the danger or not, he knows
we're extremely vulnerable to his attack in this area.

So how would the Holy Spirit lead us, in light of this
passage, if we and our spouse have different levels of desire? To the one who has the stronger need, He urges patience, kindness, and gentleness—the fruit of His work in
your life. He also counsels you to be understanding of your
spouse's feelings, especially if he or she struggles to enjoy
sex for some reason. (Men, for example, need to realize
how important it is to the wife that the *relationship* be in
good shape if she's going to welcome physical intimacy.)

Even if you're frustrated by what you consider to be insufficient physical oneness, there's *never* an excuse to be harsh, unkind, or threatening, or to force yourself on your mate. You can and should make your feelings and desires known, but only in a way that communicates complete, loving acceptance of your mate regardless of whatever conflict you have in this area—even if you never achieve the level of frequency you would most like.

To the spouse who has the lesser desire for sex, the Spirit would remind you of the passage we've just examined. You may not like to hear that message, but sometimes we need to do things we don't feel like at the time, and this may be one of those areas for you. Again, the Spirit will give you the strength to do this if you invite Him to help you. Also, we've found that when we act in obedience to God's Word, even when we don't feel like it, our feelings usually come around, later if not sooner.

The attitude we take into any situation has a lot to do with our experience of it, too, doesn't it? If we go in with a positive attitude, we'll usually enjoy ourselves; if we go in with a negative attitude, we usually won't enjoy the experience—even if everything goes well. So we encourage you to view sex as a gift that you give to your spouse, one that will be deeply appreciated and one that will strengthen your marriage. Respond to your mate as a Spirit-filled sex partner, and watch what happens!

Romance Means Relationship

Let's go back to Harry and Gwenivere and see what happens when they both tune in to the Holy Spirit.

On the way home from work, Harry talks with the Lord about his day. He takes all the pain and frustration of the day and gives it to Him. A mile or so from home, he begins to think about Gwen and the kind of day she may have had. And yes, he's already thinking about bed-time, too.

When he pulls into the driveway, he asks the Holy Spirit to help him be the kind of husband God wants him to be. Although exhausted, when he enters the house he first goes to Gwen's side, gives her a kiss, and asks about her day. As she begins to talk, he listens carefully, at the same time helping with the final preparations for dinner. Then, after dinner, he helps her load the dishwasher.

Gwen is greatly enjoying all this help and attention, and she responds with smiles and encouraging words. When the dishes are done, she wants to find out about Harry's day. He's not really keen to talk about that, espe-cially with his favorite sit-com coming on, but they stay at the table and continue to talk. Before long, as she asks questions and he answers, he finds himself enjoying the discussion.

An hour or so after dinner, this considerate husband and responsive wife make their way to the bedroom. He's raring to go sexually, while she's tired and would just as soon go to sleep. But she whispers a quick prayer and re-sponds to his overture. No fireworks go off, but his touch is not threatening and is actually rather appealing. The tenderness that has marked the evening has made its way into their love life, and they both enjoy the experience greatly.

Behind this wonderful, healthy night has been the quiet, encouraging, empowering work of the Holy Spirit. He has helped them, in this most intimate area of their relationship, to obey the Word of God and respond to each other in a celebration of their love.

He wants to do the same for you and your spouse—and He will if you let Him.

Heavenly Father,

In the Scriptures, You make it clear that my body belongs to _____ (spouse) and that _____ (spouse's) body belongs to me. We are to make ourselves available to each other in order to reduce any temptation to go outside our marriage for sexual fulfillment.

I long to have the Holy Spirit give me sensitivity and insight into the way You have made _____ (spouse). Under the control of the Spirit, I commit myself to faithfulness in my marriage relationship.

In Jesus' name. Amen.

22

Growing Together Spiritually

Throughout this book, we've been talking about the role the Holy Spirit wants to play in your life and in your marriage and how His leading and empowering can make all the difference. We've assumed that both you and your spouse are already Christians, having believed in Jesus Christ as your Savior from sin, so that you're indwelled by the Spirit and can turn to Him for that guidance and strength.

But what if your spouse is not a Christian? What if your spouse is saved but doesn't have a mutual interest in growing together spiritually? Or what if you both want to develop spiritual intimacy but you don't know how? We'll deal with each of these situations in turn.

Winning Without a Word

In 2 Corinthians 6:14-16, God had Paul write a strong warning that believers should marry only other believers:

> Do not be yoked together with unbelievers. For what do righteousness and wickedness have in common? Or what fellowship can light have with darkness? What harmony is there between Christ and Belial [Satan]? What does a believer have in common with an unbeliever? What agreement is there between the temple of God and idols? For we are the temple of the living God.

When your mate does not have the Holy Spirit by virtue of the fact that he or she is not a believer or is not walking in fellowship with the Spirit, your need for the Spirit is that much greater and your dependence upon the Spirit more critical than ever.

Our bond as Christians is the single greatest bond between husband and wife, Paul is saying. It gives us the most important things in common—the commitment to follow and become more like Jesus; the Bible as our authority for belief and conduct; the understanding that in order to obey God and fully enjoy life, we need to walk in the Spirit.

If one of the partners is not a believer, the marriage may still be good at many levels, but it won't have these vital things in common. The couple will never be able to experience spiritual intimacy, which is the greatest form of closeness.

Nonetheless, in spite of this clear counsel from God's Word, many Christians have married unbelievers. Many have become Christians after marriage and have a spouse who has not yet taken that step. If either of these represent your situation, we're confident that the Spirit will tell you that your highest priority in life should be to cooperate with Him to win your partner to Jesus Christ. Surely you don't want your mate to spend eternity separated from God. And surely you would like to enjoy spiritual unity with him or her in the here and now.

Without even speaking a word of witness,
you can lead your spouse to Jesus by demonstrating
the power and grace of God in your life.
That is best done by maintaining a gentle spirit.

But how do you communicate the gospel to an unbelieving spouse? He or she may have had a bad experience in church or with other Christians and is now antagonistic toward the whole subject. Or he or she may think that things are fine as they are, and there's really no need for God. How do you get through to this person you love in an appealing way?

God has provided an answer through the apostle Peter. The passage is directed specifically to Christian wives, but its wisdom applies just as well to husbands.

> Wives, in the same way be submissive to your husbands so that, if any of them do not believe the word, they may be won over without words by the behavior of their wives, when they see the

purity and reverence of your lives. Your beauty
should not come from outward adornment, such
as braided hair and the wearing of gold jewelry
and fine clothes. Instead, it should be that of your
inner self, the unfading beauty of a gentle and
quiet spirit, which is of great worth in God's sight
(1 Peter 3:1-4).

Without even speaking a word of witness, these verses
say you can win your spouse by demonstrating the power
and grace of God in your life. That is best done by maintaining the gentle spirit we've discussed in much of this
book. You don't have to argue, nag, or point your finger
at what your spouse is doing wrong. You don't have to be
a fighter. Loving gentleness is far more powerful than hostility. We have lost count of the number of stories we've
heard of nonbelieving spouses who were won to the Lord
by the consistent, faithful, quiet, living testimony of their
Christian partners.

By the way, this also works if your mate is a Christian
but you want to see him or her grow and give up fleshly
patterns in a specific area. Our own marriage is proof of
this. As I've said before, I tend to be a lot more aggressive
and prone to anger than Teri. She has exhibited a quiet
and gentle spirit most of her life. When she maintains that
attitude in the midst of tension, it convicts me of how badly
I'm behaving. Then it challenges me to be as submissive
to the Holy Spirit as she is so that we can resolve whatever dispute we're having without escalating the problem.
It's difficult to keep a sinful, fleshly attack going when
your spouse responds in the power of the Spirit.

When You Are Filled with the Spirit

We've talked so much about this gentle-yet-strong approach now that we'd like to spell it out a little more specifically. We'll do that by identifying the marks of a Spirit-filled husband and a Spirit-filled wife.

A Spirit-Filled Husband...

- sees gentleness as Christlike character and refuses to equate it with weakness.

- looks for ways to bring a peace and soothing atmosphere to his wife's life.

- responds with patience rather than anger when his sexual overtones aren't welcomed.

- releases his anger with self-control in the presence of God, finding healing and tranquility for his own spirit.

- guards his words and treats his wife with kindness and respect, knowing that failure to do so might hinder his prayers.

- recognizes that treating his wife harshly is dishonoring to her and is also a sign of the sinful flesh being in control of his life.

- guards his words and uses them as a way to encourage and build up his wife.

- daily and continually seeks the Spirit's leading and empowering so that he can be a husband who pleases God, growing in love, joy, peace, patience, kindness, goodness, faithfulness, gentleness, and self-control as he meets his wife's needs.

A Spirit-Filled Wife...

- looks for ways to bring calmness to her husband's heart.
- recognizes the spiritual power in her gentle and quiet spirit.
- responds to anger with her spirit of gentleness and self-control.
- knows that love, joy, peace, patience, kindness, goodness, faithfulness, gentleness, and self-control are eternal qualities that will outlast any form of physical beauty.
- makes herself available to her husband for physical intimacy, appreciating the oneness with which God has gifted them.
- daily and continually seeks the Spirit's leading and empowering so that she can be a wife who pleases God and meets her husband's needs.

If you and your spouse both want to develop spiritual intimacy but you don't know how, let us direct your attention to 1 Samuel 1, the story of Elkanah and his wife Hannah. Elkanah also had another wife named Peninnah, and she, unlike Hannah, bore him children. This fact broke Hannah's heart. She loved and served God, and she couldn't understand why He didn't make it possible for her to have children.

As we look at their situation, we see that Elkanah and Hannah continued to worship together. He took the lead, bringing his family from their town of Ramathaim to Shiloh to offer sacrifice to God year after year. In doing that, we see that he was sensitive to Hannah's spiritual condition. After providing meat from the sacrifice for Peninnah and her children, "to Hannah he gave a double portion because he loved her, and the LORD had closed her womb" (verse 5).

In verse 8, we see that spiritual intimacy also requires being open to each other. When Peninnah would taunt the barren Hannah to the point of tears, Elkanah would probe her heart: "Hannah, why are you weeping? Why don't you eat? Why are you downhearted?" And then he would encourage, "Don't I mean more to you than ten sons?"

In a similar way, John and I encourage each other in the midst of our spiritual struggles. Because of difficult circumstances and ever-increasing demands of ministry, there are times when he has felt like quitting. (John—once or twice every year!) I remind him of our calling and the fact that we're in this together. And John has done the same for me more times than I can begin to tell you. I, like Hannah, had a painful longing for a child. After praying for several years, the Lord blessed me with the desire of my heart. But during my times of disappointment, John's gentle strength and faithful support were an encouragement to me. He would always be used by the Spirit to restore perspective and peace within my heart, reminding me to claim Jesus' promise in Matthew 6:33, that if we would seek first His kingdom, "all these things will be given to you as well." And God has been abundantly faithful to that promise.

∞

Spiritual intimacy allows your spouse to stand alone before God occasionally, too. In 1 Samuel 1:9-11, Hannah felt led to go by herself to the temple and speak to the Lord. Elkanah wisely let her go. Notice that spiritual intimacy involves bringing all aspects of your marriage and family to God. In verses 19 and 20, after Hannah pledged to give back to Him the son that she hoped He would provide, she and Elkanah worshiped the Lord together. Then they went home, enjoyed intimacy, and she conceived.

The Foundation for Spiritual Intimacy

The lessons we draw from 1 Samuel 1 about growing in spiritual intimacy are these: First, worship together. Go to church together. *Pray* together—that's a must. "For where two or three come together in my name, there am I with them" (Matthew 18:20). Also study and apply Scripture together.

Second, view your marriage as a divinely ordained partnership, which is the picture we're given in Genesis and 1 Peter:

> The LORD God said, "It is not good for the man to be alone. I will make a helper suitable for him" (Genesis 2:18).

> Husbands, in the same way be considerate as you live with your wives, and treat them with respect as the weaker partner and as heirs with you of the gracious gift of life, so that nothing will hinder your prayers (1 Peter 3:7).

Third, in light of your partnership, develop a vision for how the Lord wants to use you *together*. How might He use your marriage to encourage others or bring people to salvation? How does He want you to work together in raising your children? How might He have you minister together?

Fourth, step out in faith, hand in hand, and watch God work.

Finally, if your spouse is unsaved, or if he or she is a Christian but is seemingly disinterested in spiritual growth, or if the two of you aren't at the same level of spiritual maturity, our last piece of advice is that you "pray continually" (1 Thessalonians 5:17). No one wants to see you and your partner grow together spiritually more than the Lord. So commit this vital aspect of your relationship to Him in prayer daily, asking Him to work in the hearts of both of you. Jesus taught,

> So I say to you: Ask and it will be given to you; seek and you will find; knock and the door will be opened to you. . . . If you then, though you are evil, know how to give good gifts to your children, how much more will your Father in heaven give the Holy Spirit to those who ask him! (Luke 11:9,13).

Ask. Seek. Knock. Let God show you just how much He cares for you, your spouse, and your growth together in Him through the power of His Holy Spirit.

Father in heaven,

I pray that You will make us one spiritually. By Your Spirit, impress upon each of us the need to pray together and to seek the Savior together.

Please remove from me anything that stands in the way of this kind of true intimacy. Bond us together around the Lord Jesus Christ.

In His name I pray. Amen.

23

Making Time to Hear the Holy Spirit

Arlene and Ted are your typical middle-class couple, complete with three kids, a dog, a cat, two cars, two jobs, a house in the suburbs—and a schedule that can exhaust you just from reading it. Let's take a quick look at what each of them considers a typical day.

Ted's dad had a heart attack a couple of years ago, and Ted took that as a warning sign and began to jog. Now he's up early every morning so he can get in his five-mile run, rain or shine. When he's done with that, he does his stretching exercises, showers and shaves, dresses, and goes down for breakfast. Over the meal, he buries his head in the morning paper. He's a sports fanatic, so he reads that section from first page to last. By the time he hurries out the door to drive to his job as an insurance agent, he's usually running a little late, so he starts the workday anxious and a bit frazzled.

Ted works hard at his job from the moment he walks through the office door. He prepares a letter to go to a number of clients, informing them of a change in their policies. He calls on several prospective clients, introducing himself and explaining his products. He attends a meeting with other agents and their sales manager, where they learn about a new type of policy the company is offering. He fields calls from existing clients who have questions about their coverage or premiums. He updates his presentation folder for the half-dozen sales presentations he'll make that day.

Working through lunch is par for the course, and today is no exception. Ted sometimes works into the evening, too, meeting with potential clients in their homes. He has two such appointments tonight. By the time he gets home, he'll be ready for a late dinner and maybe some TV or a little romance, hoping nobody in the family has any problems with which they need his help. Then he'll collapse into bed for a too-short night's sleep, just so he can get up early the next morning and begin the whole routine all over again.

Whew! Why does Ted keep up such a grueling pace? His philosophy is captured by the bumper sticker on the back of his car: "I owe, I owe, it's off to work I go."

Arlene is the family's chief cook and bottle washer. She gets up early to prepare breakfast and sack lunches for everybody, makes sure everyone has clean clothes, and straightens up the house a little. Then, by the time she has herself ready to face the day, she's hustling kids out the door to the school bus and herself off to work, where she's a loan officer at a local bank.

Like Ted, she works hard on the job. She's got four complex loan applications that she's trying to process as quickly as possible—checking the applicants' work histories, credit references, and so on. She fields calls from current customers, from prospective customers, from other people in the bank who know she knows the loan programs inside and out—and one from a concerned teacher who wonders why Arlene's son has failed to turn in his homework for the third time this week.

Arlene's also preparing a seminar she'll be doing in a couple of days for the finance people at area car dealerships, hoping to generate more business for the bank. Her boss has told her this is a big opportunity, and she's feeling the pressure. Today, she wants to finish designing her overheads.

Like Ted, Arlene often works right through the lunch hour. At the end of the day, she'll hustle home to get dinner ready and the kids off to, respectively, a softball game, a study session with friends, and a karate class. "It sure would be nice if Ted could take care of at least one of the kids tonight," she muses as she drives home. Then she smiles ruefully as she thinks, "But he's probably got a couple of appointments again."

By the time she's done with dinner, car ferry duties, the laundry, and paying some bills, Arlene, too, will be ready to catch the late news on TV and then collapse into bed. Romance will *not* be on her agenda as she thinks about doing the whole routine again tomorrow. Her philosophy is, "*Somebody's* got to hold this family together."

Who Has Time to Listen?

We trust you can relate somewhat to Ted and Arlene's life—if not the details, then at least the hectic pace of their days and the mind-set out of which they operate. Their schedule really is typical in modern America: frantic, non-stop, anxious, everybody going in his or her own direction, minimal communication, and no time for reflection or for developing relationships with each other or with God.

Like this couple, many of us cannot begin to hear the still quiet voice of the Holy Spirit. We have not taken the time to be still and listen; rather, we are consumed with business, allowing our frantic pace to silence His words and His work in our lives.

Teri and I have been there, too. We've talked with a lot of other couples who have as well. And we've learned that this lifestyle makes it awfully hard to spend time with God, to listen for the leading of the Spirit, and to think carefully about the choices He would have us make with His help.

Clearly, this is not a healthy situation. It means that the lifestyle many of us consider normal and routine may be antithetical to the whole idea of letting the Holy Spirit be our Counselor. If that's your situation, you may need to do some serious reevaluating, just as we did.

Let us put the case this way. If you're a Christian, would you not agree that one of your major goals (ambition, motivation) should be to please God? And while there are a number of ways to do that, in the context of this chapter, we invite you to consider 1 Thessalonians 4:11: "Make it your ambition to lead a quiet life, to mind your own business and to work with your hands, just as we told you."

*The faster we go, the more superficial
and hollow our lives become.*

Our ambition should be to please God and lead a quiet life. Notice, however, the first two words of 1 Thessalonians 4:11: *"Make it* your ambition." That's a command, which means we can do it or not do it. It doesn't happen automatically. We have to *choose* to do it and then follow through with appropriate action.

We can safely say that, with their hectic schedules, Ted and Arlene have not yet made that choice. And neither have those of us who can relate to their lifestyle. Even many pastors will tell you that they're so busy doing the work of ministry that there's nothing quiet about their lives.

Why would God command us, through the apostle Paul, to pursue a quiet life? Well, first and foremost, when we're going 90 miles an hour, how much time do we make for God? How much time do we spend in Bible reading (let alone study!) and prayer? How sensitive are we to the Spirit's gentle counsel? *The faster we go, the more superficial and hollow our lives become.* We don't pay much attention to priorities, because we have too much to do, and it all seems urgent.

In Luke 10, the Bible gives us a great picture of the contrast between someone who knew how to lead a quiet life and someone who resembles those of us in today's fast lane. It's the story of Mary and Martha, sisters and friends of Jesus whose home He was visiting. We assume Martha was the older sister, because she acted like one. Here's the account:

> As Jesus and his disciples were on their way, he came to a village where a woman named Martha opened her home to him. She had a sister called Mary, who sat at the Lord's feet listening to what he said. But Martha was distracted by all the preparations that had to be made. She came to him and asked, "Lord, don't you care that my sister has left me to do the work by myself? Tell her to help me!"
>
> "Martha, Martha," the Lord answered, "you are worried and upset about many things, but only one thing is needed. Mary has chosen what is better, and it will not be taken away from her" (Luke 10:38-42).

Now, admittedly, there may have been a lot of work to do. Jesus' disciples were probably in the house with Him, so Martha may have had 15 or more people to feed. And to her that meant just one thing: There was a job to be done! As a good hostess, she felt responsible to make her guests feel comfortable, and that included providing a fresh meal. Since she obviously held Jesus in great respect, she would want it to be the *best* meal she could offer.

One Dish Is Enough

So this go-all-out woman went to work in the kitchen, and, as she did, she could see that Mary was just sitting there, listening to Jesus teach. This made Martha irritated, then anxious ("How am I going to get all this work done on time if she won't help?"), and finally angry enough to complain about it.

Irritated, anxious, angry ... hmmm, sounds kind of familiar, doesn't it? As you looked at that story in Luke 10, did you see any joy in Martha? How about peace? patience? kindness? gentleness? No, neither did we. Not only that, but we wouldn't be surprised if, while Martha was out complaining to Jesus, some of her food was getting overdone back in the kitchen! When we're going too fast and are overcommitted, a lot of things start to go wrong, don't they? It's hard to do any one thing well when we're trying to juggle many different responsibilities. *We become ineffective as well as anxious.*

I remember one time when I watched a guy juggling knives. He would throw them up in the air and then catch them by the handles before tossing them up again. As he juggled the first two, he smiled and chatted with the audience. Even when he added the third knife, he kept up the cheerful routine.

Then he added a fourth knife, and the smile and chatter disappeared. Not even a thin smile broke his face. He was a study in anxious concentration. Why? Because he knew it would now be easy to make a mistake, and one slip could turn him into an instant blood donor!

Isn't that a good picture of our lives? We're juggling two or three major responsibilities, and we're smiling and thinking, "Hey, this is okay. Everything is fine." So then we pick up one, two, or three more because we can't say no or because we're trying to please someone (perhaps our boss, parents, pastor, spouse, or our own ego) other than God. We keep juggling away, and for a while it may seem to work. We think we're successful, and most people who observe us would agree. But now none of our responsibilities are getting the attention they deserve. Eventually, we won't drop just one of them—we'll lose them all at the same time. Isn't that the way life goes?

What Matters Most

Now let's contrast Martha's approach with what Mary did. Was Mary normally a hard worker, someone who would help her sister prepare a meal for guests? There's no reason to think she wasn't. In fact, Martha's frustration with Mary's failure to help on this occasion suggests this time was an exception.

God wants my attention more than He wants my activities, no matter how good they are or how important they seem to me.

But Mary, unlike her sister, recognized what was most important in this situation. She understood that Jesus had presented them with what might be a once-in-a-lifetime opportunity to talk with the Messiah, the Savior—to learn from Him, get to know Him, and experience His love firsthand. She wasn't so caught up in work and responsibilities, as important as they are, that she couldn't see what was *most* meaningful on this occasion. It wasn't eating, and it wasn't even showing traditional hospitality to honored guests. *The most important thing was simply, quietly being with the Savior.*

Jesus commended Mary for making that choice: "Only one thing is needed. Mary has chosen what is better, and it will not be taken away from her."

When we're too busy, one of the responsibilities that gets only superficial attention is our relationships. Our walk with God, in particular, tends to suffer first and to the greatest extent. And then comes our marriage. How about you? Have you learned the lesson that Mary and the Lord would teach us? Are you ready to make the choice to pursue a quiet life so that you can get to know the Lord, better understand His will for your life and marriage, and listen to His Spirit as He seeks to lead you in growing more Christlike?

Please believe us when we say, once more, that we know this isn't easy. I, in particular, have struggled with this. I like to go, go, go, juggling at least a dozen balls at once. I like to make things happen; I like to feel productive. It has been very hard for me to learn—and then to accept—the reality that *God wants my attention more than He wants my activities,* no matter how good they are or how important they seem to me.

Martha was *doing* something. It was important and even necessary. Mary, on the other hand, *was becoming* something. And our Lord said that Mary had chosen the better thing.

And so we ask one more time: Will you pursue a quiet life before God as your highest priority (because that's what it is), even if that requires some serious adjustments in your lifestyle? Will you learn to listen to the soft, gentle voice of the Holy Spirit as He leads you in your marriage and asks you to submit to His will? Remember, He will strengthen and empower you, doing in you what only He can accomplish.

Over time and through many painful lessons, we have learned to do these things. We're still far from perfect, of course. No one who knows us well will be nominating us for sainthood anytime soon! Yet we can honestly say that because we allow the Holy Spirit to be our Counselor, *the quality of our marriage gets better every day.*

And when we truly experience the ministry of the Holy Spirit as our Counselor, we realize that even if we had nothing this world offers, we would find contentment and joy in the fact that we know Jesus Christ.

That's what God has done for us through the Holy Spirit. That's what He wants to do for you. Will you let Him? Our prayers and best wishes are with you and your spouse as you make the choice to listen to and follow the Holy Spirit every day and in every one of your critical moments.

Dear heavenly Father,

I want my entire life to revolve around You. I want to love You with all of my heart, soul, mind, and strength. And I want to love _____ (spouse) as I love myself.

May the Holy Spirit have His way in my life. May He teach me to live in such a way as to honor Your name and accomplish the work You have given me to do—all to the praise and glory of Jesus Christ.

In the Savior's name I pray. Amen.